25- '7377

APR 27 '8

THE MACMILLAN COMPANY
NEW YORK · BOSTON · CHICAGO · DALLAS
ATLANTA · SAN FRANCISCO

MACMILLAN & CO., Limited
LONDON · BOMBAY · CALCUTTA
MELBOURNE

THE MACMILLAN CO. OF CANADA, Ltd.
TORONTO

FALSE PROPHETS

BY
JAMES M. GILLIS, S.P.

New York
THE MACMILLAN COMPANY
1925

TO
MY FATHER

CONTENTS

FALSE PROPHETS

FALSE PROPHETS

GEORGE BERNARD SHAW

I

Opinions vary as to the importance of that oddly interesting human phenomenon, George Bernard Shaw. Some profess to consider him one of the greatest of living thinkers. Others take him to be a literary trickster—a charlatan. His publishers tell us that he "does the thinking for half Europe." Indeed, the "blurb" on the jacket of one of his recent books conveys the information that "When Shaw speaks, all the world listens."

One thing seems certain. He knows how to write. His dialogue snaps and crackles and scintillates. His wit is unquestioned. He is a master, not only of paradox, but of epigram. Though he challenges the impatience of his readers by writing preposterously long prefaces to his plays, no reader skips the prefaces. They are better than the plays. The tail (if we may call a preface a tail) always wags the dog. True, Shaw can be dull. Witness *Back to Methuselah*, a play that takes three nights for one performance, and that is not only absurdly long drawn out, but also intolerably dreary. Homer sometimes nods. Shaw nods and the audience nods with him. But, generally speaking, tediousness is the last of his defects. He is diabolically smart.

His method is that of a mountebank, or a jester. His symbol is the cap and bells, his prototype the court fool. The fool was privileged to cut capers before the very face of the king. He might insult the king, mock him, mimic him, laugh uproariously at him. He might snap his fingers under the king's nose, or hit him on the head with a bladder. And, to use a clownish phrase, he could "get away with it." He was immune. *Lese-majesté* meant nothing to him. So, Shaw's trick is to insult those by whose favor he lives. He snaps his fingers in the face of his audience or his readers. He hits them on the head, sometimes with an airy bladder, more often with a knotted club. He tickles them with a rapier, and while they laugh, he sticks it between their ribs. For he is a murderous joker.

The miracle is, that, like the court fool, he "gets away with it." The English people, to whom he specially addresses himself, are perhaps of all peoples the most sensitive to ridicule. Furthermore, if they must be insulted, they would rather have any man but an Irishman do it. Yet Shaw, the Irishman, pokes fun at the English, and they laugh with him at themselves. Then he calls them asses and dolts for laughing when they should be angry, and they clap their hands with joy and admiration. He bellows at them that they are imbeciles, and they exclaim, "Isn't the fellow deliciously droll!"

But let no American call the English obtuse. If Shaw has the English hypnotized, he has the Americans bamboozled. When some of our fellow citizens attempted, a few years ago, to prevent the performance of one of Shaw's plays in New York, on the ground of its immorality, Shaw fairly shrieked his indignation. He declared that the Americans were "indecently mad." He avowed that the letters they wrote him contained "vile language," "gross suggestions," and "raving obscenity." Those who are accustomed to Shaw's habit of melodramatic exaggeration will understand that by that ferocious invective he meant merely to convey the fact that some people told him that the play in question is indecent and immoral. It is notorious that Shaw raises a wild hubbub when people disagree with him. When his indignation is aroused, the maddest exaggeration seems understatement. Take another example. Years ago, he says, he attended a meeting in a Methodist parsonage, to discuss marriage and divorce. He declared afterwards that "Peter the Great would have been shocked . . . and Don Juan would have fled into a monastery," if they had heard what was said at the meeting in that innocent parsonage. He means, probably, that some clergyman used blunt Biblical words to describe Shaw's plans for the abolition of marriage, and the establishment of polygamy.

However, certain American admirers, undeterred by Shaw's brutal and vulgar attack upon their fellow citizens, tempted his ire again by inviting him to come across the Atlantic, give a few lectures, as an excuse for a huge honorarium, and submit himself to the idolatry of the *intelligentsia*. But Shaw only volleyed back,

"Why should I go to America, the land of lynchings and of bandits? Who knows but that I should be shot down on the streets of New York, or burned at the stake in Illinois!" The Americans who had invited him chuckled at that typically Shavian pleasantry, and gave it wide publicity, just as Boswell used to hasten to record in the biography, *in perpetuam rei memoriam*, the fact that he had again been manhandled and browbeaten and bulldozed by Doctor Johnson. Johnson, of course, we can easily forgive, for under his brusqueness he concealed a heart as tender as a woman's, but if Shaw has a heart at all, no one has seen it, and Shaw will never reveal it. To cite, in passing, another instance or two of his subtle repartee: Some fond enthusiast asked him adoringly why he never eats meat. "For fear of becoming as stupid as you meateaters," was his subtly witty reply. When asked to attend the tercentenary of Shakespeare's birth, at Stratford, he answered, "I do not keep my own birthday. Why should I keep Shakespeare's?" Many anecdotes of this kind have been circulated by Shaw's press agents as a demonstration of his wit. But there are some Philistines who declare that they prove him to be a barbarian or a blatherskite.

But there is method in his brutality, as in his buffoonery. Like the court fool, he catches attention with his antics and his grimaces, his cruel witticisms and his brutal manners, and having caught attention, he shouts out his ribaldry and his blasphemy. In a letter to Frank Harris, he says, "As to myself, of course I am a ruffian. But I am only ruffianly nor-nor-west. Though it be ruffianism, yet there is method in it." "Waggery as a medium," he explains, "is invaluable. I had only to say with simplicity what I really meant and every one would laugh. I know that my opinions appear extravagant and insincere, but if the British people only knew how much I am in earnest, they would make me drink the hemlock." Elsewhere he adds, significantly, and modestly, "If a great man could make us understand him, we should hang him."

II

Of course, Shaw is not always heavy and brutal. More often—indeed almost always—he is clever and genuinely witty. I dare not deny that he is brilliant. But if one asks me to confess that Shaw is an original thinker, I demur. For it seems to me that any fairly attentive reader of Shaw must quickly detect the fact that Shavian "originality" is in reality ready-made. He follows a formula. The formula is to ridicule what the human race reverences, and to extol what the human race abominates.

For example: Mankind has always held religion to be a blessing. Shaw says it is a curse. Poverty is generally considered a misfortune, but not necessarily a sin. Shaw protests that poverty is a crime. Most men and women think that the love of a child for its mother is beautiful. Shaw calls it "horrible." We believe marriage to be a sacrament and a safeguard of morality. Shaw blatantly protests that "marriage is the most licentious of institutions." Patriotism, when genuine, is admittedly noble. Shaw declares it disgraceful.

Christians consider the martyrs to be the greatest heroes of the human race. Even non-Christians, who think the martyrs died in vain, nevertheless are wont to admire them because they died for principle and for conscience. Martyrdom, for any cause, demands a combination of moral and physical bravery. But Shaw thinks martyrdom to be proof positive of asininity. He lampoons the martyrs and grossly caricatures them. Consistently, he refused a chance to be a martyr. When the Great War was imminent, and even when it had actually begun, he was berating England, and praising Germany. But, for once, the English refused to laugh. So he first became silent and then temporarily changed his views, to conform with those of the multitude.

In view of this cowardice, it is significant that he has a particularly vitriolic detestation of St. Athanasius. He calls him "a fool, an irreligious fool, and, in the only serious sense of the word, a damned fool." Now, Athanasius was the man who stood "against the world" (*Athanasius contra mundum*) in defense of the divinity of Christ. Remembering that, we may understand why Shaw selects him, from among all the saints, as an object of special vituperation.

Take one more instance of Shaw's automatic and mechanical perverseness. Shakespeare being sacrosanct, Shaw berates him. He says that Shakespeare's plays are "full of moral platitudes, jingo claptrap, tavern pleasantries, bombast and drivel, and stolen scraps of philosophy." Even Hamlet does not escape. "The lines put into the actor's mouth to indicate to the pit that Hamlet is a philosopher, are for the most part mere harmonious platitude, which, with a little debasement of the word-music, would be proper to Pecksniff."

Shaw gibes at Shakespearean actors, and, as usual, ignoring chivalry, attacks a particularly noble and gifted woman, Mary Anderson. "The world," he says, "prostrates itself like a doormat to kiss the feet of 'Our Mary.'" But "She was no actress. She left the stage before she had served her apprenticeship." Evidently, Shaw's penchant for perversity never deserts him. He simply will not agree with the human race. But his fidelity to his formula is tiresome, and it finally becomes insufferably monotonous.

His philosophy is unmitigated pessimism. All that is, is wrong. All that exists must be destroyed. "I am, always have been, and always shall be a revolutionary writer," he says, speaking in his own name. And in the name of Tanner, in *Man and Superman*, he boasts, "I shatter creeds and demolish idols." Cato was content with a modest program. *Carthago est delenda*, Carthage must be destroyed. But Shaw cries out for the destruction of all civilization. He knows nothing good. "Our laws make law impossible. Our prosperity is organized robbery. 'Property is theft,' said Proudhon, and this is the only perfect truism that has been uttered on the subject. Our morality is impudent hypocrisy; our wisdom is administered by inexperienced dupes. Our power is wielded by cowards and weaklings. Our honor is false in all its parts. I am against the existing order."

Even so *blasé* a critic as James Huneker is somewhat

appalled (or was he amused?) by the sweeping universality of Shaw's condemnations. He sums them up:
"We are all wrong. Religious faith is modified ancestor
worship. Social life is a sham. All our glories, civic
and military, poetic and practical, artistic and mechanical, have been a huge mistake." But Huneker
has not done full justice to Shaw's pessimism. Listen
to the rest of it in Shaw's own words. "Beauty, purity,
respectability, religion, morality, art, patriotism, bravery, and the rest, are nothing but words which I, or
any one else, can turn inside out like a glove." One
can almost hear him catching his breath when he
comes to the word "bravery," and saying *sotto voce*,
"Let me see, have I left out anything?" and then adding, as a precaution, "and the rest." Let us admit
that he has forgotten nothing. He has damned everything. But that there may be "full measure heaped
up and flowing over," he continues: "Cowardice is
universal. Patriotism, public opinion, parental duty,
discipline, morality are only fine names for intimida-
tion; and cruelty, gluttony, and credulity keep cowardice in countenance." "What is fashionable society?
What does it pretend to be? An exquisite dance of
nymphs. But what *is* it? A horrible procession of
wretched girls, each in the claws of a cynical, cunning,
avaricious, disillusioned, ignorantly experienced, foul-
minded old woman whom she calls mother, whose duty
it is to corrupt her mind and to sell her to the highest
bidder."

After such a breathless outpouring of adjectives
the reader may be tempted to ask himself, "Is this

literature, or is it Billingsgate? Is the man an artist, or a blatherskite?" Whatever may be the answer, one fact is obvious. Shaw makes Schopenhauer seem like Pollyanna.

Worst of all (or should we say, to interpret Shaw's mind, best of all), there is no remedy. There is no hope. "Away with this goose-cackle about 'progress,'" he cries. "Man as he is, never will nor can add a cubit to his stature by any of its quackeries, political, scientific, educational, religious, artistic." "I do not know whether you have any illusions left on the subject of education, progress, and so forth. I have none. . . . My nurse was fond of remarking that you cannot make a silk purse out of a sow's ear, and the more I see of the efforts of our churches and universities and literary sages, to raise the mass above its level, the more convinced I am that my nurse was right." Surely, that nurse must have been a wise old crone, to know more than all the churches and universities and literary sages taken together. Since she is right, as Shaw says, no doubt we must all adopt her philosophy. But it surely is going to take the joy out of life. The world of Shaw—and of his nurse—is a world of gloom. Even the cross-grained Calvinists in *The Devil's Disciple* never imagined anything more dreary and hopeless. Shaw believes in the total depravity of the human race.

III

Being a universal iconoclast and an unmitigated pessimist, Shaw is, naturally, anti-religious. He thinks Voltaire was a credulous fool for believing that there may be a God: "I rail at the atheistic credulity of Voltaire. Even atheists reproach me with infidelity and anarchists with nihilism, because I cannot endure their moral tirades." More atheistic than the atheists, more nihilistic than the anarchists, less moral than either, surely he is a devil of a fellow. However, the atheism, the nihilism, the immoralism are good business. He admits it: "Instead of exclaiming 'Send this inconceivable Satanist to the stake,' the respectable newspapers pith me by announcing 'Another book by this brilliant and thoughtful writer.'" Perhaps, after all, he is an atheist, as he is a ruffian, "only nor-nor-west."

It must be confessed, however, that if his atheism is only play-acting, or "strictly business," he succeeds in giving a semblance of vehement sincerity to his irreligious utterances. "I loathe," he says, "the mass of mean superstitions and misunderstood prophecies which is still rammed down the throat of the children of this country under the name of Christianity, as contemptuously as ever." He calls Christianity "this religion of Salvation," which "has for its emblem a gibbet, for its chief sensation a sanguinary execution after torture, and for its central mystery an insane vengeance bought off by a trumpery expiation." His description of the origin of the Christian religion is equally distorted and even more fantastic. "Many things that man does not himself contrive or devise, are always happening: death, plagues, tempests, blights, floods, sunrise and sunset, growths and harvests and decay . . . We conclude that somebody must be doing it all, or that somebody is doing the good, and somebody else the evil—hence you postulate gods and devils, angels and demons. You propitiate these powers with presents called sacrifices, and flatteries called praises."

Shaw describes the religion of a savage. Then he attacks and, to his own satisfaction, demolishes that religion. But he imagines that he has demolished the religion of intelligent Christians. The task he sets himself is too easy. The process is simple—too simple. If he is so devilishly clever, why does he not describe the Christian religion in the words, let us say, of John Henry Newman, and demolish that, if he can. As it is, he demolishes only the religion of a Fiji Islander.

Any honest controversialist knows that if one is preparing to attack anything or anybody, one must first describe the object of attack fairly. A portrait must not be a caricature. But Shaw has no portrait of Christianity. He knows only the caricature. Perhaps there is a mite of an excuse for him. He was brought up in Irish Protestantism, and that religion is not the most lovable or most plausible of all forms of Christianity. He says that when he was a little boy, he was compelled to go to church on Sunday, and though he escaped from that before he was ten, it prejudiced him so violently that it was twenty years before he could force himself to set foot across the threshold of a church again. Evidently he had small training in religion. His parents could hardly have sent him to church (I wonder if he was taken by the pessimistic nurse) before he was six or seven. He finished his course "before he was ten." He had therefore only three or four years of churchgoing. But in that short time irreparable damage was done to his soul. "All of the vulgarity, savagery, bad-blood that has marred my literary work was certainly laid upon me in that house of Satan." Now, I have no particular zeal for the defense of Irish Protestantism, but I must confess that I faintly suspect a bit of hyperbole in Shaw's statement of the terrible things that were done to him, in three years, in that Satanical place, the church. Allowing for his usual exaggeration, perhaps he means that the minister called him a naughty boy, or that his mother spanked him for not learning his Sunday School lesson.

But ever since the tender age of less than ten, he has certainly been doing his best to "get even" with the Church. We may tolerate that. Any one may have his fling at the Church. It would seem, however, that a sense of decency, if not a natural shrinking from blasphemy, should prevent his insulting the gentle person of Jesus Christ. But not even Christ escapes him. "Setting aside the huge mass of inculcated Christ-worship which has no real significance, because it has no intelligence, there is among people who are really free to think for themselves, a great deal of hearty dislike of Jesus and of contempt for his failure to save himself and overcome his enemies by personal bravery and cunning as Mohammed did. I have heard this feeling expressed far more impatiently by persons brought up in England as Christians, than by Mohammedans, who are, like their prophet, very civil to Jesus."

Shaw must mix in queer circles if he meets people who "heartily dislike Jesus" and who express "contempt for his failure," who deny His "personal bravery" and regret that He did not practice cunning like Mohammed.

But he himself says worse things. He claims that St. Matthew makes Our Savior to be insane, and that "if we had no other documents, we should have been much less loth to say, 'There is a man who was sane until Peter hailed him as the Christ, and who then became a monomaniac.' We should have pointed out that his delusion is a very common delusion among the insane, and that such insanity is quite consistent with the retention of the argumentative cunning and penetration which Jesus displayed in Jerusalem after his delusion had taken complete hold of him." This passage pretends to be primarily a slap at Matthew, but one must be singularly obtuse who does not detect that Shaw is using Matthew as a club with which to strike Jesus.

The peculiar trick of dishonesty which permits Shaw to give a blow to Christ without directly aiming at Him, is manifest again in a passage from the preface to *Androcles and the Lion*, where Shaw is, ostensibly, arguing for the right to think and to speak realistically of Jesus. He says you may not "venture to wonder how Christ would have looked if he had shaved, and had his hair cut, or what size in shoes he took, or whether he swore when he stood on a nail in the carpenter's shop, or could not button his robe when he was in a hurry. . . . If you tell any part of his story

[13]

in the vivid terms of modern colloquial slang, you will produce an extraordinary dismay and horror among the iconolaters."

Now, I have never heard of Christians who desired to imagine all these things about the appearance of Christ. But, barring the thought of the swearing, I should not be dismayed or horrified if some devout and simple lover of Jesus Christ were curious about the intimate details of His appearance and manner. I reserve my "horror and dismay" for the man who pretends to argue for simplicity and naïveté in the consideration of Jesus, when in reality he knows that he is scoffing sacrilegiously. If a childlike saint thinks what Shaw imagines, it is piety. When Shaw writes it, it is blasphemy. The sin is not in the words, but in the mind, and in the motive.

His real opinion of Jesus Christ, apart from all subterfuge, is in this sentence from the same preface: "If Jesus had been indicted in a modern court, he would have been examined by two doctors, found to be obsessed by a delusion, declared incapable of pleading and sent to an asylum." Such is Shaw's opinion. It is not true. It is not decent. It is not smart. It is not even original. And it is blasphemy.

IV

Shaw has a strange, though, as usual, not an original idea of God. His idea is that God, or the Life-Force, is as yet unconscious of His own existence, but that He is trying to become aware of Himself. The idea is not original. It is found in many atheistic philosophies. It could be made by means of the "formula" of which I have spoken as the source of Shaw's reputedly original ideas. Indeed, he shows the manner of the working of his mind: "According to popular theology," he says, "God always creates beings inferior to Himself." Now the formula: turn the "popular theology" upside down and you have the Shavian theology. God creates beings, not inferior, but superior to Himself. "The Life-Force has been struggling for countless ages to become conscious of Himself." Man, being already conscious of himself, is superior to God. Creatures are more perfect than the Creator. The trick of being original is very simply performed, when once you have acquired the knack.

But God, as the Life-Force, blindly striving for self-consciousness, becomes a very convenient idea when Shaw comes to the exploitation of his system of morality. In the terrific struggle of the Life-Force to come to a realization of Himself, He is responsible for all the actions that take place in the mind—and particularly in the body—of man. For example, not only is one compelled by the Life-Force to marry, but one is compelled to marry a certain individual. In a particularly absurd scene in *Man and Superman*, Tanner, who fears that Ann is "setting her cap" for him, runs away from England to escape the terrible fate of marriage. But Ann pursues him and captures him in the Pyrenees. Tanner, like the tongue-tied boy in New York who was asked to give directions to a stranger, asks, "Why among all these millions of people do you pick on me?" "Why me, of all men? Marriage to me is apostasy, profanation of the sanctuary of my soul, violation of my manhood, sale of my birthright, shameful surrender, ignominious capitulation, acceptance of defeat. Why must you marry *me?*" Ann explains that she had chosen him her guardian because she wanted to marry him. The conversation continues:

"*Tanner:* The trap was laid from the beginning.

Ann (concentrating all her magic): From the beginning, from our childhood, for both of us, by the Life-Force.

Tanner: I will not marry you: I will not marry you.

Ann: Oh, you will, you will.

Tanner: I tell you, no, no, no.

Ann: I tell you, yes, yes, yes.

Tanner: No.

Ann: Yes, before it is too late for repentance.

Tanner: Yes."

Shaw elsewhere complains that if St. Matthew's Gospel is correct, Jesus was only mechanically fulfilling the prophecies, that his actions were all predetermined, that in consequence He was only an automaton. But according to Shaw's own theology, everybody's actions are predetermined, all men are automata, all men do the things predetermined for them by the Life-Force, even though those things involve apostasy, profanation of the soul, violation of manhood, and a half-dozen other calamities. If the reader of the play says, "Shaw is only spoofing," Shaw himself will answer, "I have only to say what I really mean, and every one will laugh."

There is, in the Shavian system of morality, no place

for free will. There is really no such thing as right or wrong. There is only the "biological imperative." He says as much: "In the Revolutionist's Handbook you will find the politics of the sex question as I conceive Don Juan's descendant to understand them. Not that I disclaim the fullest responsibility for his opinions and those of all my characters, pleasant and unpleasant. *They are all right from their separate points of view, and their points of view are, for the moment,* mine also. This may puzzle the people who believe that there is such a thing as an absolutely right point of view."

I mention Shaw's "system of morality," but speaking more accurately, he has no system unless it be consistently to reject the present system. In his view, the reasons that keep men and women from adultery are the same as those that keep them from eating peas with a knife. He explains that when his millennium comes, "The real superman will snap his superfingers at all man's present trumpery ideals of right, duty, honor." True, he says that "the superman will accept moral obligations beyond present human endurance." But if the future morality of the superman is foreshadowed in Shaw's plays, it will be identical with what we now call immorality. Ursula, for example, one of his characters, for whose opinions he assumes responsibility, says that if she lost her love for her husband, she would give her virtue to Marchbanks, who loves her, as unhesitatingly as she would give her shawl to a freezing beggar.

The subsidizing or professional employment of

women to be mothers is a part of the newer code. "If a woman can by careful selection of a father, and nourishment of herself, produce a citizen with efficient senses, sound organs, and a good digestion, she should clearly be secured a sufficient reward for that natural service. Whether she be financed by herself, or by the father, or by a speculative capitalist, or by a new department of, say, the Royal Dublin Society . . . does not matter. Even a joint stock human stud farm (piously disguised as a reformed Foundling Hospital, or something of that sort) might well, under proper inspection and regulation, produce better results than our present reliance on promiscuous marriage." "But mating such couples must clearly not involve marrying them . . . Marriage, whilst it is made an indispensable condition of mating, will delay the advent of the superman as effectually as Property . . . but the practical abrogation of Property and marriage as they now exist will occur without being much noticed."

Even casual "mating" is to be permitted, and no stigma must attach to it. Tanner, Shaw's particular *alter ego*, says to Violet: "Vitality and bravery are the greatest qualities a woman can have, and motherhood her solemn initiation into womanhood; and the fact of your not being legally married matters not one scrap."

Readers of Shaw will remember that such ideas as these are strewn through his writings "as thick as leaves in Vallombrosa." The man is not jesting. It is time we took him at his own valuation. It is time we ceased to consider him a harmless clown. His popularity is not due to his buffoonery. He is the darling of the "emancipated," the "advanced," and the "radicals." They take him as the prophet of a new kingdom. Reading his ideas of religion and morality, and knowing the propensities of the radicals to rebel against Christian morality, we think we understand why they fancy him.

As for us, we consider Shaw a misanthrope, a satirist without a heart, a pessimist, an immoralist, and an atheist. If it be true that he "does the thinking for half Europe," that is, if half Europe thinks with him, we may be compelled to admit that the jeremiads poured into our ears about the impending catastrophe of civilization in Europe, are well founded. But our hope for the salvation of society is bolstered up by a belief that Shaw's importance is enormously over-estimated. If it be true that "when he speaks, all the world listens," we hope it is also true that the larger and saner part of that world not only listens but condemns.

H. G. WELLS

I

One fact of primary importance, to be kept constantly in mind if we are to understand Mr. H. G. Wells, is that his genius is expansive and grandiose. This actual world, physical and intellectual, is too small for him. It cramps him. Like Alexander, he sighs for more worlds. Unlike Alexander, he is not content with sighing; he creates more worlds. And he continues the process of creation indefinitely. His readers never know what new worlds are to "swim into their ken," until they have read the latest of his semiannual volumes.

The worlds that Wells creates are, of course, incomparably better than the one created by God. The populations of Wells's worlds are as superior to the scrubby human beings who infest this earth, as we, in turn, are superior to the Cromagnon man or the Neanderthaler. His wars also are greater than ours. Our biggest was the World War. His is the *War of the Worlds*—not nations against nations, but planets against planets. Wells always "thinks big." He knows no boundaries. He is at home in the "great open spaces"—between the stars. How inept, therefore, and woefully inadequate is such a compliment as that of Anatole France, who says, "Wells is the greatest intellectual force in the English-speaking world." The "English-speaking world!" What a sphere of influence for a man whose vision comprises universes! A bungling compliment, indeed, to one whose *bête noire* is nationalism; whose immediate goal is internationalism; whose ultimate or, at least, penultimate ambition is interplanetarianism.

A more appropriate encomium for Wells is that of one who has had a better opportunity to understand him—his publisher. That discerning gentleman knows that Mr. Wells can find outlet for his exuberant genius, not merely by flitting to other worlds, but by leaping into future time. Mr. Flower explains: "Many things that Wells says are impossible. Presently they become remotely possible, and then ultimately they are achieved; the reason being that Wells is a genius a little before his time. The world catches up with him in jerks." *There* is a fancy almost worthy of Wells himself—the world hurtling through space with inconceivable speed, yet forced to take an occasional leap, a "jerk" now and then, to keep up with the more than cosmic velocity of the mental action of this prodigious man. The fancy (if it be but a fancy) is strikingly Wellsian. It smacks of science. It suggests interplanetary action. It implies earthquakes, tidal waves, and cataclysms—Wellsian revolutions. Truly a dazzling conception—the world hitch-kicking through space to catch up with Herbert George Wells.

However, even his publishers do not thoroughly comprehend the peculiar character of the genius of Wells. They advertise his books in groups, under different headings, thus:

"Mr. Wells has written
The following novels:
The following fantastic and imaginative romances:
The following books upon social, religious, and
  political questions:"

This grouping and separating are doubtless necessary, but to the unsophisticated they may be misleading. Not that I would maintain that Mr. Wells's political and historical and sociological works should be listed under the heading "Fantastic and Imaginative Romances." But I do declare that to make a strict line of demarcation between his serious books and his fantastical books is to run the risk of misunderstanding all his books. Parts of *The Outline of History* are as fanciful and as romantic as *The Food of the Gods* or *The War of the Worlds*. In his description of the first human beings, or semi-human beings, on this planet, he employed his imagination as liberally as in his description of the Men in the Moon, or on Mars. His *God the Invisible King* is as fantastic a god as his Martians are fantastic men. His prophecies of the remote future, and his descriptions of the remote past, are equally daring. His account of how the "Old Man of the Tribe" developed into God is as much a fairy tale as his story of the Brobdingnagian growth of those who ate *The Food of the Gods*.

One should, therefore, read his most matter-of-fact volumes, constantly remembering that at any moment the history, or the sociology, or the philosophy, or the theology may become wholly or partially imaginative. The element of fantasy is never long absent from any of his books. Indeed, it would be a psychological impossibility for a man with his riotous imagination to achieve a chapter, perhaps even a paragraph, without evincing the fact that the fanciful is his *mètier*. Consequently, all minute and meticulously scientific criticism of Mr. Wells's historical and sociological works would be out of the question, if not absurd.

II

But besides Mr. Wells's irrepressible *attrait* for the fanciful, there are other reasons why it would be unfair to expect scientific or historical accuracy in his work. He writes too much. He has really no time for rigorously accurate scholarship. He has been writing for thirty years, and has produced sixty volumes—to say nothing of articles for magazines, letters to newspapers, speeches, and a mountainous mass of other ephemeral stuff. No man can write so much and always know what he is writing about. True, there have been some whose literary output was even more enormous than that of Wells. Sir Walter Scott wrote more rapidly and more voluminously than Wells, but he wrote as a story-teller speaks, reckless of historical accuracy. Anthony Trollope wrote 250 words every 15 minutes by the clock. But Trollope's novels are like Ford cars—it is a mere question of human endurance and mechanical contrivance whether you get 100 or 1,000 in a given time. Arnold Bennett boasts that for some length of time he produced 500,000 words a year. Before he dies, instead of flaunting that fact, he may lament it. Here in America, we, too, have some literary Marathon champions. E. Phillips Oppenheim is said to have written 250 volumes. If he could, like Napoleon, dictate to four secretaries at once, he might have written 1,000 volumes—250 or 1,000 of Phillips Oppenheim is about the same.

But when we come to works of scholarship, there is a different story to tell. Edward Gibbon, having decided to write the history of *The Decline and Fall of the Roman Empire*, spent twelve years before publishing the first volume, and twenty-five years before finishing the work. Theodore Mommsen lived to be eighty-six years of age, and wrote only on *The History of Rome*, and immediately allied Roman topics. Janssen spent forty years preparing to write the *History of the German People*, and then he covered only two centuries. But Wells writes a *History of Life and Mankind* beginning perhaps six hundred million years ago, and coming down to the Treaty of Versailles. Any one who demands that such a work should stand the test of scientific history is cruel. Any one who thinks it accurate is gullible.

Yet the Wellsian enthusiasts seem to take the *Outline*, and indeed all of Wells's books, with solemn seriousness. Wells himself sets the example. Perhaps the most appallingly unhumorous thing he ever wrote is his statement of what he means to do even with his novels: "We are going to write, subject only to our limitations, about the whole of human life. We are going to deal with political questions and religious questions and social questions. We are going to write about business and finance and politics and precedence, and pretentiousness, and decorum and indecorum, until a thousand pretences and ten thousand impostures shrivel in the cold clear air of our elucidations." It is well that amongst all these multitudinous subjects he is not going to forget "pretentiousness."

Still, that catalogue of subjects to be treated in novels, comprehensive as it seems, is jejune in comparison with the absolute universality of knowledge he displays in *The Outline of History.* He is equally at home in Archæology, Paleontology, Biology, Painting, Poetry, Music, Anthropology, Psychology, Ethics, Comparative Religion, Theology, Numismatics, and Zoölogy. He speaks with equal confidence of Heliolithic Culture and of Tel-el-Amarna, of the Tatar language and the Rosetta Stone, of Transubstantiation and of Quadrupedal Reptiles, of the Seljukian Turks and of Sakya Muni, of the Irish Republic and the Incas of Peru. He is equally familiar with Romulus and Remus and Roosevelt. He knows the weight of the earth and the temperature of the sun; he knows the history of the Swastika sign and the habits of the saber-toothed tiger. Even the questions advertising *The Children's Book of Knowledge* would be ridiculously easy for him. He knows all about Ecumenical Councils and the Oneida Community, Maimonides and the Doctrine of Karma, the Battle of Lexington, Psychical Research, Human Sacrifice in prehistoric Mexico, Anglo-Norman Feudalism, the Hairy Ainus, Beowulf, Halicarnassus;—all are discussed with the same unhesitating omniscience. It is said that some of the statesmen at the Versailles Conference stumbled over a thousand geographical and sociological questions. Yet they had the assistance of hundreds of "experts." President Wilson himself took over a shipload of learned men. If it is a fair question, I should like to know why Lloyd George did not invite Wells to answer all questions, and so dispense with the battalions of authorities.

True, Mr. Wells himself had coadjutors. Sometimes their corrections are given in footnotes on the pages of the *Outline*. But almost always Wells disagrees with his experts. Sometimes he debates with them in the footnotes. More often he simply lets his statements stand in the text, in spite of the footnotes. He trusts that the Wellsian admirer will know whom to believe when "H. G. W." and "E. B." are at odds.

III

But the most astounding of all evidences of Wells's godlike omniscience is the fact that he knows not only historic and prehistoric facts, but thoughts that were in the minds of men so remotely prehistoric that they had not even learned to speak. Of course, he does say, "the historian can only speculate on what thoughts were in the mind of a king who lived three hundred years ago." Mr. Wells must be not only an historian, but a clairvoyant. He can tell what was in the mind of primordial man. He declares, "Something must be said about the things that were going on inside these brains of which we have traced the growth and development through a period of 500,000 years from the ape-man stage." And, bravely enough, he explains that "primordial man, before he could talk, probably saw very vividly, and mimicked very cleverly. . . . He feared the dark, no doubt, and thunderstorms. . . . No doubt he did things to propitiate what he feared, or to change his luck, and please the imaginary powers in rock and beast and river. . . . If a stick hurt him, he kicked it. If the river foamed and flooded, he thought it was hostile. . . . No doubt he had a certain amount of fetishism in his life; he did things which we should now think unreasonable, to produce desired ends. No doubt he was excited by his dreams. Since he buried his dead, and since even the later Neanderthal men seem to have buried their dead, and apparently with food and weapons, it has been argued that they had a belief in a future life. But it is just as reasonable to suppose that early men buried their dead with food and weapons because they doubted if they were dead."

So Mr. Wells runs on and on, building up paragraphs and pages of imaginary biography of men who lived a million years ago. It may be pertinent to ask how can he know all these things. For example, how can he know that primordial man was afraid in the dark? The dark, equally with the light, is the native element of the savage. The aboriginal Indian was not afraid in the dark. How can he know that primordial man kicked a stick that tripped him, or if he did kick it, why should that bit of impatience be any more significant than if a modern man slams a door, or bangs his fist upon the table, or smashes a vase with his cane when he is irritated? And the peculiar notion that primitive men may have thought that the dead were not dead—what does it signify?

Mr. Wells places an abnormal importance upon these insignificant actions, because he is adroitly building up a theory of the origin of religion. Kicking a stick implies that the stick has a soul—it means animism. Imputing anger to a raging river implies propitiation—it means sacrifice. Doing unreasonable things implies magic and fetishism. Thinking the dead not to be dead implies ancestor worship. Out of these things—animism, fetishism, propitiation, ancestor worship—Mr. Wells is going to show the origin of religion. He is, in effect, performing logical legerdemain. If his hand is quicker than your eye, he fools you.

But if you are critical and skeptical, his sleight-of-hand performance becomes a fiasco. As a matter of fact, impatience with inanimate objects, a stick, or a stone, is evidence of hysteria or neurasthenia, which are diseases of an excessive civilization, rather than of savagery. Children of civilization, whose homes are illuminated at night, are more afraid in the dark than the children of savages, who have little or no artificial light. Savages do not fear thunderstorms any more than we, perhaps less. Primitive man buried his dead because the unburied dead became intolerable. How could any man, even a savage, think the dead were not dead, when his eyes and his nose both gave testimony to the gruesome fact not only of death but of decomposition? Savages probably placed a dead man's spear on his grave for the same reason that we put cannons on a soldier's monument; they may have put food on a grave for the same reason that we put flowers on a grave. Mr. Wells's carefully contrived theory of the origin of religion is "buncombe."

But the *pièce de résistance* of his theology is the famous "Old Man Theory." I call it "his" theology, but of course it is his only at second hand, like all the rest of his theories about primitive man. He borrowed the theory of animism and fetishism from Frazer and Tylor. He borrows the "Old Man Theory" from Herbert Spencer and Grant Allen. As usual, however, Mr. Wells's description is the most graphic and picturesque. Hear him: "Certain very fundamental things must have been in men's minds, long before the coming of speech. Chief among these must have been the fear of the Old Man of the Tribe. The young of the primitive squatting-place grew up under that fear. Objects associated with him were probably forbidden. Everyone was forbidden to touch his spear or to sit in his place just as to-day little boys must not touch father's pipe or sit in his chair. Only by respecting this primal law could the young male hope to escape the Old Man's wrath." (Notice, in passing, that "Old Man" is constantly capitalized.) "And the Old Man must have been an actor in many a primordial nightmare. A disposition to propitiate him even after he was dead is quite understandable. One was not sure that he *was* dead. He might only be asleep or shamming. Long after an "Old Man was dead, when there was nothing to represent him but a mound, and a megalith, the women would convey to their children" ("convey," somehow without speech) "how awful and wonderful he was. And being still a terror to his own little tribe, it was easy to go on hoping that he would be a terror to other and hostile people. In his life he had fought for his tribe, even if he had bullied it. Why not when he was dead? One sees that the Old Man idea was an idea very natural to the primitive mind, and capable of a great development."

Great development indeed! Mr. Wells does not cease developing the idea until he has apotheosized the Old Man. The Old Man turns out to be God. Any fairly attentive reader of the *Outline*, could see that such would be the case, after Mr. Wells's first few lines, just as the inveterate habitué of the movies can tell how the story is coming out, after a hundred feet of the first reel have been run.

But even the most elementary criticism will upset the theory. It is notorious that savage people have little patience with the aged. A very considerable part of Sir J. G. Frazer's book, *The Golden Bough*, is devoted to a description of the "practice of putting kings to death either at the end of a fixed period, or whenever their health and strength began to fail." Only Christianity, and indeed a very highly perfected Christianity, leads men to be tolerant of old people, especially when the old people blither and blather and are cantankerous. Amongst savages, as soon as a man is too old to fight any powerful young fellow, the old man is knocked on the head. Mr. Wells knows that. He says so. "Some younger male will stand up to the Old Man and kill him and reign in his stead. There is short shrift for the old at the squatting-place. So soon as they grow weak and bad-tempered, trouble and death come upon them."

[30]

How Mr. Wells can say this on page 82 and yet on page 125 show the process of making a god of the Old Man, is inexplicable, except that like all legerdemain artists, he expects to divert the attention of the audience so that they shall forget what they have seen a moment ago and notice only what is before their eyes at this instant—and see that wrong.

To me it is marvelous that the most simple of all explanations of the origin of religion seems not to occur to such writers as Wells and Tylor and Grant Allen and Herbert Spencer. Robinsoe Crusoe could teach them. When Crusoe saw the footprint on the beach, he said, "Some one made it." When a savage sees a hut, or a spear, or an arrowhead, he says, "Some one made it." When he sees a mountain, or an ocean, or a tree, or a waterfall he says, "Some one made it." That is the origin of belief in God, and religion. But the explanation is too simple for the learned. They must have something more recondite. If they are both learned and romantic, they must have something bizarre. If they are learned and romantic and "scientific"—like Wells—they must build an argument from a stick, or a spear, or an "angry" river, or an Old-Man-that-Bullies-the-Tribe. Meanwhile the fact remains—as big as a mountain or an ocean,—that men from the beginning have believed in God because they instinctively understand the fundamental scientific law of cause and effect. The mountain had a Maker, the ocean had a Maker—God. A simple, but sufficient theology.

Now, for fear that some may imagine that Wells despises the savage for making a god, let me hasten to explain that he believes that *every man* should make his own god. As for himself, Wells sometimes has a God, again he has no God, and then he has a God once more— it depends largely upon external circumstances, and the effect produced upon his mind by world events. Before the war he had no God. During the war, he had a God. Now, since the Treaty of Versailles, and the dismal state of Europe resulting therefrom, Wells once more has no God. At least, one cannot find any God in his latest works. But he may have a God again at any moment. In this matter, as in others, one can never tell until one reads his latest book. Like some other excessively rapid thinkers, he drops his convictions as swiftly as he acquires them. It is part of the evolutionary theory that growth and development demand the elimination and extinction of forms of life proved to be inadaptable. So of ideas and convictions. They were useful yesterday, they are a drawback to-day. Drop them. They may be helpful to-morrow. Pick them up again. Truth comes and goes. "Fly away, Jack; fly away, Jill. Come back, Jack; come back, Jill."

Still, Mr. Wells did declare at one time, with an appearance of permanent conviction: "Religion is the first thing and the last thing, and until a man has found God and been found by God he begins at no beginning and he works to no end." That sounds like the first page of the Catechism. A Christian reader might well cry "Bravo!" But wait and see what Mr. Wells means by "finding God." He means that literally and truly you must discover God for yourself. I have *my* God, and you must have *your*

God. My God is no good for you—your God is no good
for me. I must not take your God, or St. Augustine's
God, or St. Paul's God. I must not even take Jesus
Christ's God. I must discover God for myself. Wells
thus works a metaphor to death. Naturally we refuse
to follow him. There is, indeed, a sense in which every
man must "discover" his own God, but if I attempt
literally to make my own God, I fear I shall make a
botch of the attempt. Even Plato and Aristotle
and Socrates, who all believed in God, had some very
curious elements in their concept of God. For Christians, the God of Jesus Christ will suffice. His God
is good enough for us, and better than any we could
make for ourselves.

Wells bungled his God even more than Plato or
Aristotle. In fact, he has made two gods. There is
a god in your heart and a god beyond the stars. The
two are in conflict. The god in your heart is a rebel
against the other god. The high God, Who is Almighty and Omniscient, does not interest Wells. His
god by preference is the god of the heart, who is not
omnipotent and not omniscient, not the Creator of
the universe. Strangely enough, though not omnipotent nor omniscient, he is omnipresent. But his
power is limited. He has not yet come to his strength.
Wells sometimes calls him "The Old Experimenter."
He is a god who is doing the best he can. We have all
heard the "agnostic's prayer," "O God, if there be
a God, save my soul, if I have a soul." Wells's prayer,
I imagine, is somewhat like that, and yet different.
"O God, help me! Or, at least, help me if you can!"

Students of the history of religion will easily recognize Wells's two-god theory. It is Gnostic, and Manichæan. It suggests Ormuzd and Ahriman, or Creator and Demiurge. Wells confesses that he got it from Shelley. Shelley may have got it from the Persians. But the idea of an omnipresent but not omnipotent God is a little something of Wells's own. That is possibly what he means by discovering his own God.

IV

For Christianity, Mr. Wells has only vituperative contempt. As usual, the contempt is based on ignorance, for he shows "an ingenious unfamiliarity with the creed of Christianity." With characteristic inconsistency he sometimes praises Christ and sometimes questions His very existence. He says in *First and Last Things,* that it is a matter of no importance whether Christ ever lived or not. Granting that He did live, Wells thinks that the Christ of the Gospels had no very definite teaching. But after Christ, St. Paul, a man of subtle intellect and considerable education, elaborated the Gospel into a theological system. This system was then further developed in the first four centuries and was codified and crystallized by the time of the Council of Nicæa, A. D. 325.

It is not my intention to discuss at length the extent to which these views are either false or fallacious. I desire but to indicate that this cut-and-dried explanation of the origin and growth and corruption of the Christian religion was, as usual, borrowed, not invented, by Wells. There is nothing in his concept of Christianity that was not written by the Tübingen school seventy years ago. But, old or new, original or borrowed, the explanation is unscientific, in that it does not account for the continuous existence of the Christian religion. A convinced evolutionist, like Mr. Wells, should understand that a system which becomes crystallized in the fourth century cannot be a living organism in the twentieth century. Systems are like species; when they are no longer vital they yield in the struggle for existence. When they yield they die and become extinct. Crystallized systems are like fossil remains. Mr. Wells should know that the Church is not extinct and not fossilized. Only a few years ago he wrote that the twentieth century was destined to see an enormous revival of Catholicism. Perhaps he has already forgotten that prophecy. A man who cannot remember on page 125 what he said on page 82, can hardly be expected to remember in 1924 what he said in 1920. But it is surprising that at the moment he penned that prophecy, the thought did not flash through his brain, "Let me see—crystallized at Nicæa in the fourth century? Yet due for an enormous revival in the twentieth century? is this good evolutionistic doctrine?" But pshaw! Why am I constantly forgetting my own warning that his serious writings are not serious?

Before dropping the question of Mr. Wells's attitude toward Christianity, let me show by a few quotations not only how hopelessly prejudiced is his view, but how thoroughly lacking he is in humor when he deals with what arouses his "vituperative contempt." At least half a dozen times during his consideration of Christ and Christianity in *The Outline of History,* Wells proclaims that he is disinterested, that he is no theologian, that a history is not a theological treatise, and that he will avoid theological controversy. Then, close upon the heels of these ingenuous protestations, he writes sentences like these:

"It is a matter of fact that in the gospels all that body of theological assertion which constitutes Christianity finds little support."

"Christ did not say a word about the worship of His mother Mary, in the guise of Isis, the Queen of heaven."

"All that is most characteristically Christian in worship and usage, He ignored. Skeptical writers" (Heaven forfend that Wells should be thought skeptical) "have had the temerity to deny that Jesus can be called a Christian at all."

"There was nothing in His teaching that a follower of Gautama Sakya might not receive very readily, nothing to prevent a primitive Buddhist from also being a Nazarene, and nothing to prevent a personal disciple of Jesus from accepting all the recorded teaching of Buddha."

The Crucifixion was attended by "foolish stories of physical disturbances. We are told that a great darkness fell upon the face of the earth, and that the veil of the temple was rent in twain. . . . It is difficult to believe nowadays that the order of nature indulged in such meaningless comments."

"The gospels contain the teachings of Jesus on the

one hand, and the glosses and interpretations of the disciples on the other."

"Was Jesus God? It is not the function of the historian to answer such questions. The reader is referred to the Athanasian creed for the exact expression of the mystery. To Gibbon he must go for a derisive statement of these controversies. The present writer can deal with them neither with awe nor derision. They seem to him, he must confess, a disastrous ebullition of the human mind entirely inconsistent with the plain account of Jesus preserved for us in the gospels."

"These attempts to say exactly how God was related to Himself were presumptuous and intellectually monstrous; nevertheless we are bound to recognize that beneath these preposterous refinements of impossible dogmas, there lay often a real passion for truth."

He is not a theologian. The *Outline* is not a theological discussion. He is an historian, and it is not the function of the historian to answer such questions. But he *will* say that miracles of nature are "foolish stories" and "meaningless"; that Jesus ignored all that is most characteristic of Christianity; that the gospels are partly His teaching and partly the interpolations of ignorant men; that Christ was no Christian, that St. Paul was no Christian, that a primitive Christian and a primitive Buddhist are identical, that creeds are "presumptuous and intellectually monstrous," and that the divinity of Christ is but one of a number of "preposterous refinements of impossible dogmas," which are "disastrous ebullitions of the human mind." It is a great satisfaction to know that

Mr. Wells recognizes the limitations of the historian, and that he so modestly confesses his ignorance of theology!

I accuse Mr. Wells of lack of humor. I may as well speak my full mind and accuse him of lack of honesty. In view of his violent attack upon Christianity, his protestations of neutrality, so oft repeated, can be nothing less than hypocritical. When he says "We shall treat Jesus of Nazareth as being what He appeared to be, a man. . . . If the light of Divinity shine through our recital we will neither help nor hinder it," does even his most devoted admirer imagine that Wells's mind is still unconvinced as to whether his narrative shall show the divinity in Christ? When he further proclaims that he will discuss Christ impartially, as "we have already done in the case of Buddha, and as we shall do later with Mohammed," we Christians are frank enough to say that to treat Christ with as much aloofness and scientific cold-bloodedness as we treat Buddha or Mohammed is for us an impossibility. Our emotions and our feelings for Christ are such that we cannot consider him dispassionately. But neither can Wells treat Christ, or Christianity, dispassionately. Even so loyal a Wellsian as Heywood Broun, in his "American Foreword" to Sidney Dark's *Outline of Wells*, is sensible enough to see, and to say, "Wells is no neutral. Even in his novels, he is a passionate partisan!" If he knows that, his protestations of neutrality are hypocritical. If he doesn't know it, some one ought to tell him that all the rest of the world knows it.

For Catholicism, as one might surmise, Mr. Wells

has the same "vituperative contempt" as for Christianity. And the same "passionate partisanship" against it. The limits of this discussion do not permit me to accumulate evidences of his constant anti-Catholic prejudice. I shall give but one example of it, an example that will sufficiently demonstrate his spirit. He says in Chapter XXXV (or XXXIV in the one volume edition) of the *Outline:* "It is certain that the Catholic Church through its schools and universities opened up the prospect of the modern educational state in Europe." So far so good. But wait! "It is equally certain that the Catholic Church never intended to do anything of the sort. *Its purpose in spreading education was the subjugation of minds!*" [1]

Readers of G. K. Chesterton's *Orthodoxy* may remember his description of the bewilderment that came upon him, while he was still an agnostic, from reading the self-contradictory ideas of the enemies of Christianity. He was given to understand that "not only had Christianity the most flaming vices, but it had apparently a mystical talent for combining vices which seemed inconsistent with each other." Mr. Chesterton says that this was the lesson he learned by reading all the agnostics "from Huxley to Bradlaugh." But Wells has discovered a still more "mystical talent" in Catholicity, the talent of *identifying* virtues and vices.

---

[1] I have italicized the last sentence. If colors were used in this book, I would illuminate it. I consider that sentence to be a perfect gem of anti-Catholic bigotry.

V

It is a curiously invariable fact that those who treat Christianity and Catholicity with "vituperative contempt," have also indifference or disdain for the virtue of purity, and a fondness for "advanced" ideas on sex morality. I do not mean that we should impute personal immorality to Mr. Wells. Like G. B. Shaw, he may, with his inevitable inconsistency, practice virtue while condoning vice, and be a living model of *bourgeois* respectability while advocating a more than Bohemian recklessness of morals.

I say that he condones vice. In *The Research Magnificent* William Porphyry Benham travels much, leaving his wife solitary at home. In her husband's absence she "receives the embraces" of another man. Now we might grant Wells the right to record the wife's infidelity without moralizing. It is the current opinion that although a novelist is like God, in that he creates men and women, he is unlike God in that he is unconcerned about what his creatures do. But Wells is not content to stand aloof. He defends the action of Mrs. Benham. "A woman" (he explains) "cannot wait about like an umbrella in a stand."

And in a more recent novel, *Men Like Gods*, he explains, through the mouth of Mr. Barnstaple, that the women in his new Utopia associate sexually sometimes with one man, and again with another—or others. "Why!" exclaims Father Amerton (who, as every one knows, is a caricature of the late Father Vaughan), "That is free love." Barnstaple, with hot indignation, retorts, "That's the trouble with you priests. You are nasty-minded." And he continues to vituperate Father Amerton. "You are a dirty priest. What you call Christianity is a black and ugly superstition, a mere excuse for malignity and persecution." When Mrs. Benham practices adultery, Wells defends her. When Father Amerton protests against free love, Barnstaple calls him "dirty." Is Wells an artist, standing aloof from his creatures, letting them act in accordance with their characters, or is he a "passionate partisan"?

Connected (at least in the minds of Christians) with the question of sex morality is the question of motherhood. We consider motherhood a sacred vocation. Wells considers it a gainful occupation. He is an ardent and indefatigable advocate of state endowment of motherhood. He makes of motherhood a profession—like law or medicine—or a business—like stenography or bookkeeping. Years ago, he declared with vigor that there is no more reason why every family should rear its own children than there is why every family should conduct its own gas house or water works or electric power house. He favored the segregation of children in large asylums. They were to be brought up by the State. Now, apparently, he concedes that, in some cases, at least, children may be brought up in private, but under the supervision of the State. He has the details of the system fairly well worked out. "The amount to be paid" (to the mothers) "should vary with the financial standing of the home. People of that excellent class which spends over a hundred a year, ought to get about that much from the State.

People of the class which spends five shillings a week per head on them, should get about that, and so on. To endow only poor and bad-class mothers, would be supremely idiotic. . . . If the supply of babies rises too fast, diminish the payment." [1] This from a man who calls a priest "dirty" because he believes that love and marriage between one man and one woman is a sacrament!

VI

But sex morality is comparatively a small matter. Mr. Wells has lost the fundamental basis of *all* morality, the distinction between good and bad. He makes Mr. Polly say (and Mr. Polly is generally understood to be an authentic though rather ludicrous exponent of Wellsian philosophy), "One starts with ideas that things are good and things are bad . . . I've always been the skeptaceous sort and it always seemed rot to me to pretend men know good from evil." It is Wells's idea that the right and wrong of any action can only be judged by its immediate results, a principle that will ruin morality and civilization.

Since that is his philosophy, what wonder that Wells, like so many other false prophets and false moralists, is growing more and more deeply pessimistic? That an evolutionist can despair of the world is a mystery. It would seem that the theory of evolution might be summed up in three words, "Onward and Upward." But the man who wrote *The Outline of History* as a thesis to demonstrate that the progress of the world

[1] *Social Forces in England and America*, Harper, N. Y., p. 272.

and of man is as inevitable as the attraction of gravitation, is in despair about the world and man and life. He speaks of man's life contemptuously as "this little stir amid the slime, a fuss in the mud." [1] He thinks the world a "very sinister and dreadful world." He is convinced that all civilization is crumbling. If these things be so, the much vaunted evolution of the earth and of the race was hardly worth all the pain and all the time it has taken. If it ends now, the ultimate result is a fiasco, or a tragedy. But we who do not consider evolution a key to all mysteries, and a solution of the Riddle of the Universe, are not despondent. We believe in God—not an impotent God who is only doing the best He can, but a God Who has ten thousand times set the world right again when everything seemed wrong, a God Who can and will bring the race out of the morass into which it has so willfully strayed.

It would scarcely be fair to say that Wells, though a pessimist, has entirely abandoned hope. There is, he admits, one last chance for civilization—Education. In a famous phrase he declares that the fate of civilization depends on the outcome of the "race between education and catastrophe." Specifically, he urges that "every one should know three or four languages well, German, French, Italian, English, and should also have more than a smattering of Russian, or Hindustanee or Chinese." The prophet of a new world, the creator of one Utopia after another, having before his eyes Germany, the most highly "educated" nation that

---

[1] In "The Undying Fire," cf. Mr. Newman Flower (his publisher), in the *Daily Mail*. Quoted in *Literary Digest*, Mar. 27, 1920.

ever existed, and believing that Germany deliberately brought about the most enormous catastrophe in history, still thinks that the world can be saved by "education"!

The truth in the matter is obvious, so obvious that Wells and other false prophets must exercise considerable ingenuity to avoid seeing it. The truth is this: Education will not avert catastrophe. Nor will eugenics and the endowment of motherhood. Nor will the League of Nations. Nor will any other artificial device save mankind. The only force that can rehabilitate the world is the institution that Wells treats with "vituperative contempt." The only Savior of mankind is the One Whom Wells pretends to consider coldly and impartially, the One Whose actual existence or non-existence Wells says is a matter of no moment— Jesus Christ.

SIGMUND FREUD

I

Sigmund Freud turns psychology upside down. He studies not what the mind knows about itself, but what it does not know, or, at least, does not know that it knows. He is concerned not with states of the conscious self, but with the unconscious. For him the normal is not the key to the abnormal; rather the abnormal is the key to the normal. The immediate subject matter of his science of psychoanalysis is not human nature, but the uglier side of human nature. André Tridon (principal popular exponent of Freud in America) emphasizes this fact with a particularly horrible illustration. He says: "The sculptor who decorated the Basle Cathedral with a statue of a beautiful woman, the reverse of which is covered with a struggling mass of snakes, toads, lizards and other slimy and creeping creatures, has well symbolized our human nature." It may be doubted that the sculptor intended to symbolize human nature. Perhaps he meant to symbolize sin—a special kind of sin. However, it is significant that the psychoanalysts look upon human nature as originally and essentially, if not incurably, loathsome. It is their first principle that even the most innocent and beautiful human traits cannot be understood except by the investigation of those elements of our nature that are beastly. The old psychology concentrates its attention upon the fair face of human nature, considering what is vile to be merely a corruption of what was fair, and being consequently content to have it hidden away. Psychoanalysis insists upon turning the statue around, and fastening its gaze upon what is ugly, saying, "This is our normal, natural state; the beautiful is artificial and abnormal."

In spite, however, of the peculiarities and paradoxes and revolting features of psychoanalysis—perhaps because of them—the new science has caught the fancy of the multitude, has greatly influenced modern literature, and through literature is presumably affecting modern life. Whence comes the attractiveness of so repulsive a science, it would be hard to say. One writer [1] thinks that the war has made us morbid. "Another complex left behind by the war," she says, "is the obsession of abnormal psychology. I do not mean to say that there was no such obsession visible in our literature before—far from it. But the war vastly extended its scope and authority. This was inevitable. For war itself is a pathological state of society. . . . Surrounded by abnormal conditions without, men's minds have turned inward upon themselves and fixed upon primitive 'instincts' at the core of being, with sex as a center."

Perhaps, indeed, the war is partly to blame for the vogue of psychoanalysis. We blame the war for everything evil. But a morbid interest in abnormal mental conditions would have developed, war or no war. It

[1] Helen McAfee, "The Literature of Disillusion," *Atlantic Monthly*, August, 1923.

seems to be an adjunct of our peculiarly neurasthenic type of civilization, a consequence of the mental and moral enervation that follows upon a long and luxurious peace, rather than upon an invigorating war. Warriors grow rough and hard and cynical, but not morbid. However, it is true that (to resume Miss McAfee's words), "the forms this obsession has taken in literature . . . constitute nearly all the 'new' fiction, poetry, and drama that has been written in the last five years . . . This imaginative literature of twisted subconsciousness has engaged a large majority of the finer minds among the young writers." In view of this undeniable vogue of psychoanalysis, a scrutiny of its principal features seems to be necessary.

II

It cannot be denied that the primary postulate of the new science has a certain fascination. This primary postulate is that the human mind has never forgotten anything. All that we have thought and done and suffered, and that seems to have been forgotten, remains locked up in a deep and hidden corner of the mind, which Freudians call the "Unconscious." "The Unconscious Mind," says Fielding,[1] "is the reservoir which receives all the accumulations and experiences and impressions of the personality. . . . It is that region of the mind where are deposited and have been since birth every sight and sound that we have perceived, and every feeling that we have had; in fact, everything that has happened to us, however trivial."

[1] William J. Fielding, *Psychoanalysis, the Key to Human Behavior.*

[47]

Indeed, some psychoanalysts go further, and maintain that the "Unconscious" still remembers everything that happened either to ourselves or to our ancestors, back to Adam, and—yet more—that our unconscious self treasures, not only as a memory (a forgotten memory, if we may speak paradoxically), but as a source of all our mental and physical activities, the instincts and tendencies and passions, and vaguely, even the facts in the life history of the beasts whom the evolutionists take to have been our primitive for-bears. To illustrate: A very familiar dream is that of falling through space, trying desperately and vainly to grasp something to impede our fall, awaking with a crash as we hit the floor. The psychoanalysts explain that such a dream is a reminiscence of the time when our ancestors slept in trees, and, sometimes falling, tried in vain to grasp a branch with their paws or tail, awaking with a crash as they hit the ground. It is a long time since we slept in trees, but we still remember that fall!

Since some psychoanalysts reject the theory of an everlasting memory from aboriginal times, as a fanciful elaboration of the teaching of the master, let us express the Freudian idea in the authentic Freudian manner. Deep down below the surface of our being, lie lurking the instincts and the passions, not only of our barbarian and savage ancestors, but of the beasts that were *their* ancestors. These tendencies, instincts, "urges," have been repressed by man, as a condition of his civilization. Though repressed, they remain, unknown, unrecognized, but potent. They are the mainspring of all our actions, the stimulus of all our thoughts. Ignorantly, we ascribe our thoughts and actions to causes that lie upon the surface of the mind. The real causes are below, in the Unconscious. Amongst these denizens of the mental underworld, there are certain feelings or "ideas" which dominate. These are called "complexes." Each "complex" is a rallying point of hosts of primitive repressed emotions. The "complexes" are always in a condition of rebellion. They are restrained and kept below by a warden who guards the gate that separates the unconscious from the conscious mind. The guardian of the gate Freud calls the "Censor." The "Censor" is himself one of the "urges"—the self-protection "urge." In spite of his prosaic title, the "Censor" is a courageous fellow, and his function is heroic. It is his self-appointed task to prevent any "urge" from rising to inconvenience us or to endanger or embarrass us in the society of the civilized. He rules the other "urges" like a lion-tamer. He cracks his whip over them. They may snarl and growl, but none the less they slink and cower. Be it remembered, that the function of the "Censor" is distinguished from that of the consciously exercised will-power by which one knowingly restrains his evil tendencies. The "Censor" acts automatically and secretly. The master whom he is protecting does not even know of his existence.

In passing, need we remark that such psychology as this is far removed from the old science that was to most of us as tedious and tiresome as economics or mathematics? Indeed, this is not psychology. It is romance. It is poetry—of a kind. No wonder it has caught the fancy of the crowd. No wonder it has been eagerly seized by the novelists, and that the reading public, long weary of the everlasting repetition of old ideas, has welcomed psychoanalysis as an interesting and stimulating novelty.

Not all the "urges" are savage. Some of them are merely contemptible, or dirty, or shameful. There are coyotes as well as wolves, hyenas as well as lions, toads as well as tigers, in the Unconscious. There are complexes of hate and fear and shame and cowardice, as well as of savagery. There is, most important and most insistent of all, the *libido*, or sex urge. Freud himself explains that *libido* does not mean merely sexual craving, but the general impulse at the base of the emotional life. Still, the *libido*, narrowly understood as the sex urge, seems to absorb an enormous amount of the attention of most Freudians.

But to return to the "Censor": It seems that in spite of all his zeal for our welfare, he is really the cause of all our trouble. Our diseases, mental and moral and physical, particularly the neurasthenia and the hysteria that characterize modern civilization, are due to the repression of the "urges." The "Censor" is too efficient. He "inhibits" and suppresses only too successfully. There results a psychic strain on the individual, a great deal of wear and tear upon the mental constitution. In the opinion of at least some Freudians, it would be better if the wild beasts could occasionally overpower the lion-tamer, break down the barrier, and escape into the upper conscious mind; better if the slimy reptiles could sometimes glide past the warden and creep up into the light. For the constant repression of the urges—though it be necessitated by civilization—is unnatural and produces all manner of abnormal conditions.

III

So far the theory. Now for the practice of psychoanalysis. Let us suppose a patient suffering from illness —particularly a mental or a moral illness (which may, perhaps, produce its effect on the physical organism). He is morbid, overnervous, excitable, irritable—not indeed insane, but suffering because the equilibrium of his powers is upset, or because their activities are badly coördinated. It is the duty of the practitioner to delve down into the patient's "Unconscious," discover which particular complex is causing the trouble, drag it up to the conscious mind, show it to the patient—in a word, to banish it by exposing it to the light. For the beasts are, after all, more imaginary than real. They owe their strength largely to the fact that they are concealed. They are dream beasts that vanish with the light of day.

Naturally, the practitioner will not be able to drag them out in a moment. The process is generally slow. For, according to the hypothesis, the region of the mind that is to be explored is the "Unconscious." The patient does not even know his own complexes, and how can he be expected to tell what he does not know? He would deny that he has "complexes," and the "Censor" is only too anxious to keep the hideous or shameful secret, not only from the investigator, but from the patient. But the psychoanalyst, by stimulating confidence, by inducing the sufferer to talk freely about his inner and outer life, and particularly by watching and recording certain apparently insignificant but telltale habits of speech or of action, finally discovers the hidden cause of the ailment.

These apparently "insignificant habits" are such things as a slip of the tongue, a slip of the pen, a little absent-mindedness, a mannerism, an occasional forgetfulness. For example, a patient in a hospital says to a visitor,[1] "When I was rushed to the hospital in the middle of the night, to undergo a serious operation, it happened—as if by accident—that the man whom I consider to be the greatest surgeon in the city was here. I am a lucky man. I owe my life to him." Just then the surgeon entered the room. The patient attempted to introduce the surgeon to the visitor, but he had suddenly forgotten the name of the man who had saved his life! Obviously, it was embarrassing to all three persons, but particularly to the patient, since, as he said afterwards, "For years I have known that doctor's name as well as my own. And to think that I should forget his name at just such a moment!" To the layman such an incident has little significance. He considers it simply an instance of temporary lapse of memory. But the psychoanalyst declares that it tends to show that subconsciously, or unconsciously, the patient, in spite of his fine protestation of admiration and gratitude, really hated the surgeon. Freud says, "We forget names because they have an unpleasant unconscious connotation." Tridon further declares that "the name of a pleasing man or woman does not have to be repeated

[1] The present writer was the "visitor."

to us. It is immediately engraven on our memory." On the other hand, "I frequently found it necessary to refer to my notes to get the names of persons who had caused me much trouble."

Tridon gives scores of instances [1] of what he considers significant absent-mindedness. For example, a stenographer during a whole week was constantly omitting the letter "s" from all her work. Her employer finally asked her, "Whom have you decided to drop, whose name begins with "S"? The girl blushed and confessed that she was about to jilt her sweetheart, whose name was Smith!

Again, two students are talking of a football game. "I see," says one, "that Amherst beat Brown." "You mean," says the other, "Dartmouth beat Brown." "I *said* Dartmouth!" "No, you said Amherst." Psychoanalysts would have us believe that the first student disliked Dartmouth, and so unconsciously substituted for it the name of another college.

A man takes a wrong train, by mistake. Intending to go to Bridgeport, he gets on a train that stops only at New Haven. Therefore, unconsciously (strange as it may seem!), he hates Bridgeport!

The textbooks of psychoanalysis are crowded with cases like these. These accidents are supposed to be of scientific value. But the Freudians must permit us to indulge a little skepticism about the importance of these apparently insignificant slips of the tongue or the mind or the memory.

[1] *Psychoanalysis: its History, Theory and Practise.* Huebsch, N. Y., 1919, also, *Psychoanalysis: Sleep and Dreams.* Knopf, N. Y., 1921.

Freud tells a particularly curious story of a little accident, from which he draws a big conclusion. The wife of a lawyer in Vienna, on the anniversary of her marriage, cut a finger on her left hand. Now, in Austria, it seems, a lawyer, *Doctor juris*, is called "a doctor of the right," whereas a physician, *Doctor medicinae*, is called a "doctor of the left." The lady had been engaged to a physician before her marriage to the lawyer. Her marriage turned out unhappily. Therefore, says Freud, an unconscious impulse led her on her anniversary to cut her left hand! She still loved the doctor of medicine! It really is too bad that Sherlock Holmes is dead, or doomed to inactivity. Here would be a new and fertile field for his genius.

IV

However important may be the deductions from absent-mindedness, after all, "the royal road to the unconscious is the dream," said Freud. It seems that when we sleep, even the vigilant "Censor" takes a nap or, at least, grows a little drowsy. But the "urges" never sleep. They watch their chance and burst through into the upper mind. The result is a dream. Inhibitions are released, and the brain is filled with images which may be horrible, ugly, or nasty. In every case, a dream is the fulfillment of a desire. It is the protest of nature against the artificial restrictions of civilized life. Furthermore, the psychoanalysts declare that in sleep we *always* dream. We may speak of "dreamless sleep," but there is no such thing. And there are no trivial dreams, no unmeaning dreams.

Every dream is significant. It needs only to be interpreted. Consequently the practitioner cross-questions his patient most thoroughly about dreams.

But here enters one of the most curious features of the entire theory of psychoanalysis. Dreams are said to be frequently, if not always, symbolic. Although the "Censor" relaxes his vigilance when we sleep, he never quite loses his hold upon the rebellious "urges." To get by him, even as he drowses, they must disguise themselves. Hence, in the brain of the dreamer there comes not a plain picture, but a symbol of the desire of nature. It behooves the psychoanalyst to be acquainted with the meaning of all symbols, such as boxes, and shoes, and birds and daggers, and fish, and wagons, and trunks, and swords, and ovens, and tunnels, and falling teeth, and trampling horses, and ponds of water, and various beasts, and colors, and ten thousand others. The textbooks of the art of psychoanalysis are veritable dream-books. The augurs of ancient Rome who took the auspices by examining the entrails of animals or the flight of birds, had, it wou'd seem, a comparatively simple task compared with that of the modern practitioner of psychoanalysis. To lessen his difficulty, symbols are listed and their significance noted in the manuals of the art. If one doubts the meaning of any symbol, his first resort is to "look it up in the dream-book." If it is not listed, he may pretty safely assume that the symbol, whatever it is, has sex significance. Every symbol that I have named, and a thousand others, have reference to sex or sexual passion, or sex perversity.

If the patient asks the obvious question—"How can a symbol mean anything to me in a dream, since it means nothing to me when I am awake?"—Tridon answers, "The unconscious mind is older than the conscious mind, and speaks an older language." The unconscious mind remembers what the conscious mind never knew. For example, the significance that ancient or prehistoric man attributed to an old boot has not been forgotten by the unconscious mind. The modern maiden who so thoughtlessly throws a boot at the bride and groom is blissfully ignorant of the meaning of her action, and would be terribly embarrassed if she were told. But her unconscious mind knows. The unconscious mind also remembers, even to-day, the symbolic significance of rice in the obscene ceremonies of ancient Egypt, even though the conscious mind has never learned it. As of boots and rice, so of all the other symbols. They all meant something, epochs and ages ago, and the unconscious mind remembers what they meant. Has it not been explained that the Unconscious forgets nothing that has happened or been known or thought or imagined since Adam—and before?

If I hasten over this matter of the sex symbolism of dreams, it is because the subject is rather unsavory. But be it noted that the manuals of the art of psychoanalysis do not dismiss it briefly. It is the very basis of their science. Indeed, it may truly be said that sex interest, even sex perversion, is the principal stock in trade of the psychoanalyst. Perhaps that is one of the reasons why the textbooks of the science were crowding even novels off the tables of the booksellers, until the novelists, in self-defense, took up the subject. "All excitement," says Fielding, "is primarily sexual. In the strictly Freudian sense nearly all instincts, emotions and actions are motivated primarily by an unconscious sex urge." True, he explains: "Sexuality is not the equivalent of sensuality but denotes the fundamental instinct which is at the very root of the emotional life, called the *libido*." Even with this explanation it is remarkable that Freud and his followers can find no better word than *libido*, "lust," to denote excitement that is "sexual but not sensual." As for the sweeping statement, "All excitement is primarily sexual," must we say that the "rooters" at a football game, the ruffians who snort and howl and bellow at a prize-fight, the crowds that shout in the streets when soldiers go off to war, as well as little children who shriek at their play, are all activated by an unconscious sex urge?

But there is one subject, even more unpleasant than that of dreams and their significance, that must not be entirely ignored. We must at least make mention of the famous Œdipus Complex, and together with it the Electra Complex. To state plainly what these things mean would be disgusting. Let it suffice to recall that, in Greek mythology, Œdipus killed his father and married his mother, and that Electra conspired with her brother and killed her mother to avenge her father. A boy, therefore, who has been too much loved by his mother, and is psychically deranged in consequence, is said to possess the Œdipus Complex. A girl who is so madly in love with her father as to be jealous of her mother, possesses an Electra Complex.

Perhaps it was this miserable perversion of natural affection that led Bernard Shaw to say, with his usual mad exaggeration, and his usual reckless indiscrimination, that mother love is one of the seven capital sins. Tridon declares: "Affectionate mothers probably wreck the careers of more children than indifferent ones." Fielding says, more moderately but still rather offensively, that "the man who carries the mother image in his Unconscious so that it dominates his actions is a typical neurotic." D. H. Lawrence, who is not only the author of particularly obnoxious psychoanalytical novels, but has written perhaps the nastiest of all manuals of psychoanalysis, sees a shameful meaning even in the glance of the Child in His mother's arms, in the Madonnas of Leonardo, Botticelli, and Filippo Lippi. And he declares, in a burst of excessive honesty, that "Incest is the logical conclusion of the ideals (of psychoanalysis) when these ideals have been carried into effect. You must admit incest as you now admit sexual marriage, as a duty even. Psychoanalysts will never openly state this conclusion, but it is the conclusion which, willy-nilly, every analyst must come to." He adds, "*All* inhibition must be wrong, since inevitably in the end it causes neuroses and insanity."

At least some other psychoanalysts agree with the overfrank D. H. Lawrence. For example, a man named Hans Bluher, a teacher in the *Gymnasium* (High School) of Steglitz in Germany, taught that the worst form of unnatural vice as practiced by the pagans of ancient Greece, should be restored under Christian civilization, and he actually put his theory into practice amongst his own scholars, until the nefarious practice was discovered and stopped by the authorities.[1]

V

After narrating such excesses and enormities as these, it may seem quixotic to attempt to find any good whatever in the theory or practice of psychoanalysis. Still, a purified science of psychoanalysis may be possible. It is conceivable that the art of investigating the roots of human nature may be improved and rendered harmless. The facts that such an investigation brings to light are not all repulsive. Digging beneath the surface of the human mind we may find, not toads and lizards, but treasure. William James used to write much about the "Hidden Powers of Men." If Freud had not been so obsessed with the idea that everything at the root of our being is vile; if, in his penetrating analysis into human nature, he had discovered these "untapped reservoirs of power" of which James used to speak, and if he had taught us how to tap them, he might have been what his admirers claim—a discoverer and benefactor as great as Copernicus or Newton or Harvey. He might have been for the human race like a prospector who says to a farmer, "You think that the only value in your land lies on the surface—your crops. But beneath the surface there is enormously greater

[1] Preuss, in *Fortnightly Review*, St. Louis, August 15, 1922.

wealth; deep down beneath your grain and your corn there is an inexhaustible supply of *oil*."

There is generally some truth and some wisdom even in the most perverse philosophies. Underlying the theory and practice of psychoanalysis is some of the virtue of the Catholic Confessional. As far back as the third century of our era, Origen advocated confession because it "externalizes the rottenness." The *Following of Christ* advises sinners to "spit the poison out." And all the world is aware that "Open confession is good for the soul." Even apart from sacramental absolution, the practice of confession may be beneficial. Talking out our sins, if it be done in the proper spirit, is as helpful as talking out our troubles. Therefore, if it were possible to provide a class of practitioners of psychoanalysis, well-trained, discreet, accustomed to mental and spiritual discipline, and sincerely interested in morality, the new art and science, if such it be, might be a boon to the human race, second only to the immeasurable boon of the use of the Sacrament of Penance.

But the literature of psychoanalysis and our experience of so-called "psychologists" give us little reason to hope for the existence of such a body of trained and virtuous psychoanalysts. Ninety per cent of the books and tracts on psychoanalysis are evidently written by persons of little spiritual insight, and even the best of the books, including those of Freud himself, contain many bizarre and fantastic ideas, much pseudo-science, and not a few suggestions that, from the point of view of Christian morality, are monstrous. Until the psychoanalysts tone down their doctrines and purify their notions of ethics, until they expurgate the animalistic theories that so permeate and vitiate their systems, we shall be wary of them.

A host of practitioners of applied psychology, working upon the theory that all psychic activities and all psychic aberrations are to be explained by the animalism of man, will do the race enormous harm. The habit of concentrating attention upon sexual irregularities is particularly noxious. Through many hundreds of years of experience in dealing with souls and with sins, the Catholic clergy have learned that it is wisdom, as far as possible, to ignore, to forget, the meaner and nastier tendencies of the animal part of our nature, and to emphasize the higher things of the spirit. "Let these things be not so much as mentioned among you, as becometh saints," said St. Paul, speaking of sins of the flesh. Any intelligent observer of human nature knows that it is the peculiar power of the passion of lust to thrive upon any attention given to it. Therefore, the Catholic Father Confessor in all cases advocates brevity in the confessional, and particularly demands of morbid, hysterical, and scrupulous persons that their story be short and swift. He considers it folly to dwell upon evil tendencies; to sit down and discuss them in minute detail, over a long space of time, he would consider criminal, perhaps even sacrilegious. Yet it seems to be the method of psychoanalysis to probe and penetrate and investigate and discuss things that might better be briefly confessed and summarily forgotten.

The Freudian psychology appeals especially to

neurasthenics. It plays into their hands. Nothing so irritates them as a brusque "pooh-pooh, you are not sick," from their family physician or their spiritual adviser. Nothing so flatters them as to be told, "You are sick with the most terrible form of sickness, your 'Unconscious' is ill. Let us sit down together and talk it all over. Say all that is in your mind. Take plenty of time—hours, weeks, months." Receiving such mad advice as that, they sigh and say, "This is the man who understands me." The last state of that neurasthenic will be worse than the first. From that moment, he will read books containing descriptions of strange and curious psychic ailments, he will learn a new vocabulary for describing his diseases, he will see himself in Strindberg's plays, and Sherwood Anderson's poems, and D. H. Lawrence's novels. All erotic literature will be to him an explanation and an interpretation of his "neuroses" and his "psychoses." Psychoanalysis is a boon—and a curse—to the one who loves to describe himself as a "nervous wreck."

Furthermore, it is unwise, and in most cases immoral, to permit a man to shirk responsibility for his own sins or his own overdeveloped passions. Putting the shame upon one's ancestors, or upon Adam and Eve, is bad enough, but to exculpate ourselves because we have, presumably, inherited the ugly passions of some prehistoric Pithecanthropus, is a dangerous expedient. Yet in manuals of psychoanalysis may be found again and again such statements as these: "When men and women sacrifice honor, fame, home, family, and everything else to indulge a passion for some individual of

the opposite sex, the potency of unconscious passion
once more has its sway. . . . The millions of years of
indulgence . . . rise above the few thousands of conscious reasoning power."

This is only a new form of an old excuse; and excuses
for sin, old or new, are not only cowardly, but demoralizing. It is good Christian doctrine that one should
stand upon his own feet, stiffen his backbone, set his
jaw firm, call upon the almighty power of God, fight the
good fight, and win the battle, and not go whimpering
about the passions of the cave man of thousands of years
ago, or of some "missing link" of millions of years ago.

Finally, it seems a tragic mistake, particularly in
these days, to overemphasize, as psychoanalysts do,
the "ravages wrought by repression." Just now we are
not suffering from too much self-control. The fault
of the age is self-indulgence. We do not live in a world
that is barren of variety and of amusement. We have
ten thousand ways of "letting off steam." Our civilization is not overly puritanical. We could stand a
little more austerity. If civilization is in danger of
breaking down, it is not because it is too rigid, but
because it is too loose. The psychoanalysts, with their
constant insistence upon the theory that the restrictions necessary for civilization are the cause of all our
woes, physical, psychical, and moral, are doing a very
poor service to civilization.

CONAN DOYLE

I

Sir Arthur Conan Doyle feels confident that he is the proper kind of man to investigate psychical phenomena. He presents his own credentials: "All my life I have been an open-air man. I have boxed and played football. I have driven my own car in an international automobile race. I spent my youth on a whaler in the Arctic seas. I have been often under fire." So he asks with assurance, "Would you pick me out as the kind of man who loses his critical faculties in a medium's dark room?" [1]

To that question, the answer is, "Probably, yes!" The qualifications of an athlete may, perhaps, guarantee a man against hysteria, but they do not safeguard him from being duped by charlatans. Athletes are generally simple, sincere, unsuspicious. Their "critical faculties" are usually undeveloped. They are notoriously not of the skeptical sort. Rather they are inclined to be superstitious. They believe in "luck," and "hoodoos," and "mascots," and "jinxes." Some of them, like Sir Arthur, even believe in fairies. The two men in all America who could be most easily deceived by a medium, at a séance in the dark, are (I would say, at a venture) "Babe" Ruth and Jack Dempsey. To tell the truth, an "open-air" man is out of his element in the

[1] *American Magazine*, September, 1922.

close atmosphere of a medium's chamber. Therefore, Sir Arthur's list of his many accomplishments is interesting and edifying, but not convincing, to one who seeks an expert in psychical research.

It is significant that, in summarizing his accomplishments as an investigator of mysterious problems, Sir Arthur has omitted the fact that he is the creator of Sherlock Holmes. There are those who imagine that the author of good detective stories must himself be a good detective. But the cruel fact is that Sherlock Holmes, prince of story-book detectives, would be a failure if assigned to run down a criminal in real life. No one will be silly enough to ask Conan Doyle, on his next visit to New York, to apply the method of Sherlock Holmes to the discovery of the murderers of "Dot" King, or Louise Lawson, or Joseph B. Elwell. We have a hundred of these murder mysteries in the great city. If Conan Doyle could solve but one of them, the police would forgive him for all the contempt he has poured upon their "profession" through the lips of the omniscient and infallible Holmes. Until then, he must be patient with us if we continue to doubt that either athletic prowess or the power to create an imaginary detective will enable one to distinguish fact from fraud at a spiritualistic séance.

Nor am I particularly impressed with the notion that scientists or psychologists make good investigators of mediums. With all due esteem for Professors Lodge, Hyslop, Wallace, Flammarion, Richet, and the rest, I think if I were going into a dark room to witness spiritistic happenings, I would rather have a policeman than a professor for companion. And when I say "police-man," I do not mean the usual "cop," whom one sees on the street—big, burly, bovine, sauntering along his beat, jovially greeting his friends, twirling his "billy" playfully, whistling a bit of a tune, chucking babies under the chin—in a word, a Conan Doyle sort of police-man. Crimes are done under the nose of such as these. Boy bandits, and even girl bandits, snap their fingers in the face of these slow-moving, slow-thinking, good-natured fellows. No, when I say "policeman," I mean one of another type, a natural-born sleuth, cold-blooded, cynical, skeptical, with long experience in the devious ways of crooks. Still better might be a newspaper re-porter, an habitué of the police courts, who would give his eyeteeth for a good story and ten years of his life for a "scoop." This is the sort of fellow who cares nothing for the etiquette of the séance parlor, or the ritual of the trade; who is not too dignified to sneak under the table to see what the medium is doing with her feet, and who will, if he gets a chance, feel around in the dark for the electric light switch, and throw it on at the most embarrassing moment. It was one of this ilk who first exposed the famous Palladino, greatest of modern "mediums," who had played her tricks unde-tected by a hundred learned but gullible professors.

Best of all, in the séance chamber, would be a "ma-gician." But it seems to be considered unsportsman-like to have a magician at hand where a medium is performing. Not long ago, *The Scientific American* invited a group of investigators to be present at the testing of a medium. Among the guests was Harry

Houdini, the celebrated "magician." He turned out to be an *enfant terrible*. The medium was detected in fraud, and when the Committee, doubtless with excellent reasons, delayed announcing that fact, Houdini impetuously called up the newspapers and "spilled" the story, to the apparent discomfiture of the experts. The Chairman announced that Houdini would not be invited again.

Yet Houdini has a right to be on such a committee. He has been studying "psychic" phenomena for over twenty-five years. He has, on occasion, played the part of a "psychic,"—as a hoax. At an entertainment aboard an Atlantic liner, he answered Theodore Roosevelt's question, "Where was I last Christmas?" by drawing a map of "The River of Doubt," and indicating the precise spot, much to the amazement of the ex-president, who at that time had published nothing about his South American trip, and had shown no maps to any one. Just by way of good measure, the map was signed by William T. Stead, who was lost on the Titanic. "Is it really done by spirits?" exclaimed Mr. Roosevelt. "Yes," said Houdini, with a wink. In all seriousness, the famous magician has asked seven men, now deceased, who were interested in psychic research, to send him a message from beyond, if possible. He has received none. He stands ready at any time to duplicate with legerdemain any "spiritistic" phenomena. Between Conan Doyle, the big, good-natured, soft hearted, open-air Irish athlete, and Houdini, the wizard, I should choose Houdini as one who would retain his "critical faculties" in the dark room.

II

However, this is all *a priori*. Let us rather consider a few facts which demonstrate the unscientific, credulous nature of the man who has made himself a propagandist of spiritism. Just before embarking on a recent tour to Australia and New Zealand, he had a sitting with a medium, "good Evan Powell, who came down (from London to Devonshire) to give me a last séance." "I had the joy," he continues, "of a few last words with my arisen son. He blessed me on my mission and assured me that I would bring solace to bruised hearts. *The words he uttered were a quotation from my London speech at which the medium had not been present, nor had a verbatim account of it appeared anywhere at that time!* It was one more sign of how closely our words and actions are noted from the other side."

This is doubtless very touching. But might not a moderately critical reader ask if the medium could have had a messenger at the London speech? Is it unthinkable that a London medium, had, in anticipation of a séance, obtained a few sentences from a public speech by the most famous of all propagandists of spiritualism? These simple questions seem not to have occurred to the one who is so sure of his "critical faculties"! I will not, however, insist further upon this pathetic incident of the alleged colloquy of the bereaved father with his departed son. Any further discussion of such a subject would be cruel. When Sir Oliver Lodge exposed his broken heart, in the pitiable account of his communication with his boy Raymond, who, like Doyle's son, was killed in the Great War, one friendly reviewer said, "Patriotism stifles the voice of criticism." So, when Conan Doyle, with most engaging disingenuousness, though with doubtful propriety, invites the world to listen to his talks with his dead boy, we may only say, "Sympathy stifles criticism," and pass on to cases where a deep and sacred emotion is not involved.

Sir Arthur, however, seems to have no scrupulous regard for domestic privacy. He tells that he has talked, not only with his son, but with his mother, from beyond the grave. And he says, with the innocence of an imaginative child, that he has heard angels singing "Onward Christian Soldiers" in his children's nursery. Also, he does not hesitate to tell rather intimate things concerning himself. It seems that he suffers occasionally from insomnia. But he has a remedy —prayer. Now, it is only too scandalously true that prayer sometimes acts as a soporific (a great many persons will testify that they fall asleep over their prayers), but it seems that when Conan Doyle prays for sleep, he is actually anæsthetized. He says that, on such occasions, he experiences "a very distinct pungent smell of ether, coming in waves from the outside."

He has also prayed against mosquitoes. But, rather oddly, he prayed only that his face be spared. In consequence, he says, "Though my hands were like boxing gloves, and my neck was all swollen, there was not a mark upon my face." The story reminds me, somehow, of a conversation I heard between a mother and her boy: "Didn't I tell you to wash your face?" said mother. "No, you didn't," answered sonny; "you only told me to wash my hands." It would seem that Sir Arthur's benefactor from the spirit world ought not to have taken the poor man's prayer with such cussed literalness.

III

Sir Arthur has a very curious notion about the soul. He explains that "the soul is a complete duplicate of the body, resembling it even in the smallest particulars of outline and color. In life the two are commingled. At death they divide. The eye cannot see the soul (generally) after the division, but the camera can." Apparently, then, Doyle's famous spirit photographs are not of risen bodies, but of souls which after death retain the form and color of the body, and not only of the body but of the clothing. Sometimes, it would seem, the clothing is suspiciously anachronistic. Sir Arthur himself records that at a séance in Australia, an ancient Assyrian hand wore a modern starched cuff. But, ordinarily, the style of the clothing, as well as the shape of the body, is as unchanging as the soul. Some of us will not be any too well pleased to learn these facts. Think of wearing collars and cuffs, and trousers (apparently the same pair), for all eternity. As for the form of the body, some of us are not so proud of our figure that we would care to keep it forever. To tell the truth, we have grown careless about the "daily dozen"; we have convexities where there should be concavities, and *vice versa*. We are stooped and round-shouldered, and even a trifle lopsided. We are like G. K. Chesterton's man who had a funny shape—"too fat in one place, too thin in another." But hitherto we had hoped to get a more graceful body in the resurrection. It is disconcerting to learn that we shall retain for eternity the shape we have when we die.

Conan Doyle claims that he has "the most wonderful psychic photographs ever shown in the world." He has exhibited them at his lectures everywhere. But when he was challenged by a New York photographer, who declared that he could produce, by trickery, equally fine "spirit" photographs, Doyle paid no attention to the challenge. Mrs. Doyle, speaking for her husband, declared, apparently with some warmth, that Sir Arthur would not accept the challenge or "that of any other publicity seeker." This is odd, because in his book, *The Wanderings of a Spiritualist*,[1] he relates that he did accept a challenge from a photographer in Sydney, N. S. W. If in Sydney, why not in New York? If he favors some unknown in the antipodes, why not accept the challenge of the well-known and perfectly reputable *Scientific American*, which offers a large money prize for *any* spiritistic phenomenon or any "spirit" photograph produced under test conditions?

The lofty scorn with which Sir Arthur declares that, while he has great esteem for the editor and the scientists connected with *The Scientific American*, he cannot bring himself to apply for the prize because their offer "serves only as a summons for swindlers," is rather un-

[1] Collin's edition, p. 160.

convincing. Sir Arthur should be eager to show that there is at least one who is no swindler. He should be able to produce an honest and efficient medium. And I dare say that if his chosen medium passed the test, the victory would do the cause more good than trips around the world and lectures to miscellaneous and indiscriminating audiences. Meanwhile, until he, or some one equally well-known, produces photographs under test conditions, for some accredited scientific society, skeptics will continue to think that his collection, no matter how "wonderful," has been palmed off on him by adepts at substitution. If a prestidigitator can remove our watch from our pocket without our knowing it, even though we are looking directly at him in broad daylight, if slate-writing charlatans can exchange our slates for their own, before our own eyes, it is not inconceivable that a medium can substitute trick photographic plates before the eyes of a man who sees fairies, hears angels sing, prays for ether to come in the window to put him to sleep, and obtains immunity from mosquito bites on his face by the miraculous intervention of an unnamed supernatural power.

IV

But, indeed, Sir Arthur has not merely an unscientific unconcern about fraudulent mediums. He actually defends, excuses, and champions some who have been detected in fraud. At a séance held in London, at the suggestion of Mr. Wilson Young of the London *Saturday Review*, Mr. Young became suspicious that the various spirit voices were proceeding from the mouth of a person present in the flesh. He reached out his hand in the dark and touched the broad end of a trumpet that had been placed upon the floor before the lights were turned down, but that seemed to be floating through the air as the various voices were heard. When Mr. Young touched the large end of the trumpet, he felt that it was supported at the other end. At the same moment, the trumpet was left in his grasp. He lifted it carefully over the head of one of the sitters, and placed it on the floor behind Conan Doyle's chair. *There were no more spirit voices that afternoon.* The séance was abruptly closed, and the lights were turned on. As the party left the house, Mr. Young explained to one lady who had been particularly excited and moved by the spirit voices, "I must tell you that the voice you heard was not your mother's but the medium's." Sir Arthur was furious, and wrote a long letter of protest to *The Saturday Review*, accusing Mr. Young of "conduct unbecoming a gentleman." "It is really your want of knowledge and experience," he said, "which you are exposing. If you would appreciate that this is a deep matter, and that it is impossible that a tyro could solve at first glance what has baffled so many thousands, you would have gained the beginnings of wisdom! Even mental want of harmony can spoil a séance." Rather a stinging rebuke for one who simply touched the trumpet and put it back on the floor where it had been placed before the room was darkened! But the mediums, like Sir Arthur, are very easily offended. They make their own conditions; they turn out the lights; they demand that the sitters shall not stir from their chairs;

and if any one so much as mentally disconcerts them, they call off the séance. A professional magician would be ashamed to take such advantage of his audience.

If we compare the timidity of Sir Arthur with the cold-bloodedness of truly scientific investigators, we may see why he will have nothing to do with the latter. Here, for example, is a newspaper account of one of the sittings at the office of *The Scientific American*. A certain George Valentine, one of "the best mediums in the country," was trying for the $2,500 prize offered by *The Scientific American:*

"The staff proceeded in the matter with a certain practical coldness. They set luminous buttons on the walls, invisible from Mr. Valentine's chair, but visible from certain others. If a body passed in front of the button, naturally its light would be obscured. They also placed the medium's chair above an electrical apparatus which caused a light to show in another room so long as a person remained sitting in the chair. If no one sat in the chair the light would go out. Stenographers in the same adjoining room took down the ejaculations of spirits and the words of the medium, watched the light connected with the chair and timed the periods when it failed to burn, etc. The buttons were obscured, the light went out, fifteen times. The voices of spirits and the failure of the light to burn coincided. The implication was that in order to do his work as a ghost-maker the medium had to leave his chair, although he had promised not to do so. He did not win *The Scientific American* prize."

This is the kind of investigation which Conan Doyle

avoids, and which he stigmatizes as "liable to serve only as a summons to swindlers." To the uninitiated it would seem that such a séance would be a deterrent of swindlers, after the first two or three have been exposed.

V

On his visit to Australia, Sir Arthur was particularly impressed with the work of an "apport" medium named Bailey. It is Bailey's specialty to transport all sorts of objects, large and small, old and new, living and dead, from one part of the globe to another, instantaneously and invisibly. They "pass through the walls, and are precipitated down upon the table." Bailey has produced, from the ends of the earth, according to Sir Arthur, "eighty-seven ancient coins, eight live birds, eighteen precious stones, one hundred Babylonian tablets, with legible inscriptions in Assyrian, some of them cylindrical, with long histories upon them, one Arabic newspaper, one leopard skin, four birds' nests, one shark, as well as unnumbered Chinese school-books, mandarin's buttons, tropical birds," and other curious and exotic things. Only a few familiar objects seem to be missing. Those who remember the old "sleight-of-hand" performances will miss the rabbits, and the roses tumbling out of nowhere, filling up the stage and overflowing into the orchestra pit. Nor is there any mention of grand pianos or elephants floating over the heads of the audience. Indeed, the animal exhibit might have been more complete. For, although a shark was present, no "goat" is mentioned. Perhaps, after all, there was a "goat" at the meeting, but naturally Sir Arthur would not recognize or record that fact.

It seems that Bailey was exposed in France in 1910. "The *curious*," says Sir Arthur, "will find the *alleged* exposure [Italics mine] in 'Annals of Psychical Science,' Vol. IX." But the exposure in Paris naturally does not interfere with his performances in Melbourne. There are ten thousand miles between the two places.

Besides, Sir Arthur says that the exposure was unsatisfactory, and he explains why. Amongst the objects produced in the Parisian test were two birds, supposed to have come from some remote continent. But a bird-seller in Paris deposed on oath that he had sold Bailey three such birds in a cage. Bailey denied that he had bought the birds, and supported his denial by declaring that he knew nothing of the French language and that he had no French money. This satisfies Sir Arthur, and his satisfaction is corroborated by the fact, as he says, that "only two birds were produced, and no cage. Where was the other bird, and where was the cage, if the bird-seller spoke true!" This annihilating query quite demonstrates that the open-air man had not lost his "critical faculties" in the passage to Australia.

Doyle took one of the Assyrian tablets home to London, and showed it to experts in the British Museum. The experts declared it a forgery, and said that quantities of such "fakes" are produced by certain Jews in a suburb of Bagdad. But this information did not disconcert Sir Arthur. He explains that "to the transporting agency, it is at least possible that the forgery, *steeped in recent human magnetism,* is more capable of being handled than the orginal, taken from a mound."

Surely, Conan Doyle is a resolute believer. His faith remains unshaken in the face of exposures and forgeries. He not only tolerates but defends a lying medium, or at least he condones the lie, because, as he says, "one has to remember that physical medium-ship has no connection, one way or the other, with personal character, any more than the gift of poetry."

A tendency to tolerate and to forgive a lying medium, and a willingness to trust the liar again and again, is noticeable in other, and more "scientific," investi-gators than Conan Doyle. Even the greatest mediums have been detected in fraud. But certain members of psychical research societies continue to trust them. In addition, they sometimes show a curious mixture of guilelessness and ingenuity in explaining why they still believe a liar. They say, for example, that a medium in a trance does not know and therefore is not responsi-ble for any fraud that may be committed; or they introduce the scientific hypothesis of dual personality, and declare that the good personality must not be blamed for what the evil personality does, any more than Dr. Jekyll should be blamed for the doings of Mr. Hyde; or they explain that mediums are generally simple persons, perhaps peasants, who have little or no realization of the meaning of a lie or the seriousness of deceit. Most strangely, they are disposed to believe a medium when he testifies in his own behalf, but to discredit his testimony when he makes a confession of guilt. The Fox sisters, for example, deceived two continents and set the world by the ears for a whole generation. Then they publicly and solemnly swore that all their phenomena were fraudulent. Later they retracted the confession, even though it had been made under oath.

A medium named Blackman, says Richet, told how he deceived Gurney, Myers, Podmore, Sidgwick, and Barrett, the greatest investigators in the history of psychical research. The celebrated "Eva" (Marthe Béraud, Richet's particular *protégée*) told a lawyer that she had tricked at the Villa Carmen (Richet's home). Later on she denied this. Eusapia Palladino created a big stir amongst professors, until, to use the strong phrase of F. Scott Schiller, she suffered "a very handsome and complete exposure." [1] A famous American medium, Keeler, who for years was a favorite with congressmen and senators and ambassadors at Washington, received "annihilating exposure."

"Miller, Bailey, Mrs. Williams, Eldred, Sambor, and A. Roth have all been exposed," says M. Richet. [2] "Eldred had an armchair in which he had collected a whole arsenal of trick 'properties.' The photographer Boursnell, although he had the support of W. T. Stead, was convicted of cheating. So, likewise, was the French photographer Buguet, though simple-minded persons, even after his trickeries had been exposed, persisted in believing in the genuineness of these phantoms. Mrs. Williams was unmasked at a séance in Paris; there were found on her, various things used to simulate

---

[1] Supplement to *Encyclopedia Britannica*, Art. "Psychical Research."
[2] *Thirty Years of Psychical Research*, p. 456.

phantoms, as in Eldred's case. Sambor's case is very strange; one of the friends of Petrovo Solovovo was actually his accomplice, though seemingly an honourable man. According to Grasset, Ebstein made up a phantom with a painted doll.

"Bailey, who claimed to make 'apports' of living birds, was caught at Grenoble buying the flame-coloured birds that he was supposed to bring from India by magical means. Maddock was condemned for cheating. I was able to show up Anna Roth who brought concealed flowers. Before the séance she weighed one hundred and sixteen pounds, but only one hundred and fourteen afterwards; the weight of the flowers she brought was two pounds. Maxwell cites the very suspicious cases of Mrs. Wood and Lemb.

"Haxby cheated impudently. I could heap up cases if need were."

Conan Doyle replies to such facts as these with an act of faith. He thinks that a medium, even though a liar, may produce *bona fide* phenomena, just as an immoral poet may write genuine poetry! And M. Richet explains, again and again in his large volume, *Thirty Years of Psychical Research*, that deceit does not destroy the validity of psychical phenomena, and that it merely proves nothing but the mental frailty of mediums. And he adds naïvely, "A curious volume might be written on the pseudo-confessions of mediums." To me it would seem that mediums once proved fraudulent are scientifically useless forever after. A liar may lie at any moment.

Sir Arthur has a curious and novel view, not only

of the lies of mediums, but of lying in general. In the same volume wherein he tells the story of his Australian séances and lectures, he speaks of De Rougemont, the celebrated traveler, who is thought by many to be a French Munchausen. Doyle doubts that De Rougemont deserves such a reputation. And he explains innocently, "Either he is a liar, in which case he is, beyond all doubt, the most realistic writer of adventure since Defoe, or else he speaks the truth, in which case he is a great explorer. I see no possible avoidance of this dilemma, so that *whichever way you look at it, the man deserves credit*." Now this conclusion is evidently very kindly, and it makes us admire Doyle's charity. But we must insist that such serene indifference to the question of whether a fact is a fact, indeed, or only a bit of romantic imagination, is quite out of place in an investigator of psychic phenomena. An investigator should have a fierce love of truth and a fiery hatred of a lie.

VI

But why labor the proof of Conan Doyle's childish simplicity and credulity? Let us have only one more instance of it. He was speaking at a luncheon given in his honor by the spiritualists of London. The company numbered two hundred and ninety persons, chosen, obviously, because of their sympathy with the cause of spiritualism. In the midst of his address, Sir Arthur, "with a sudden impulse, called upon those in the audience who were prepared to swear that they had actually spoken face to face with friends or relatives who had passed over, to stand up and testify." Two hundred and fifty out of the two hundred and ninety arose. "It was wonderful," says Doyle. But even the gentlest skeptic might ask, "How did the other forty get in to a 'hand-picked' spiritualist luncheon party?"

Like all sincere spiritualists, Doyle is not only gullible; he has lost all sense of the ridiculous. For example: he permitted to be printed in the newspapers of the world the following sentences spoken to him, he says, by Lord Northcliffe's spirit:

"Only a wave of spiritual reform can save the world." "The American people are too busy." "When men lose wisdom, they invite disaster."

These banalities remind us of nothing so much as Hamlet's report to Horatio of what his father's ghost had told him, "There's ne'er a villain dwelling in all Denmark but he's an arrant knave," and Horatio's reply, "There needs no ghost, my lord, come from the grave to tell us this."

VII

Finally, let us see what Sir Arthur has to say of the Christian religion,—for, of course, he confronts Christianity at every step, in his "Wanderings," physical and mental.

It is his opinion that "Christianity has stagnated and degenerated." [1] And the stagnation and degeneracy occurred very early; "The process was completed about the end of the third century." [2] By that time (to

[1] *Wanderings of a Spiritualist*, p. 31.
[2] *Ibid.*, p. 136.

change the metaphor) "the living thing had set into a petrifaction." Now the reason of the stagnation, degeneracy, and petrifaction was that, "at that time there was a conflict between the priest with his ritual, and the medium without any. The conflict split the early Christian Church and ended in the complete victory of the ritual, which meant the extinction not only of the medium, but of the living, visible, spiritual forces, which he represented. Flowers, music, incense, architecture all tried to fill the gap, but the soul of the thing had gone out of it. . . . Only now does the central fire begin to flow once more through all the ashes that have been heaped above it."

How the Christian Church contrived to exist for six-teen centuries after "the living, visible, spiritual force became extinct," and "the soul had gone out of it," and it had become "petrified," and "covered with ashes," Conan Doyle does not explain. It is a pity that he suggests such a question without stopping to answer it. But now, he says, the life is coming back and the flame is being fanned. One might hope that the newer and purer form of religion would emphasize the main feature of primitive Christianity. But unfortunately the original and essential Christian teaching, the divin-ity of Jesus Christ, is not to be revived. For, says Doyle, "The spiritualistic movement, so far as it is an organized religion, has taken a purely Unitarian turn. That is, spiritualists value Christ as a great psychic, but they are Unitarians with a breadth of vision which includes Christ, Krishna, Buddha and all the other great spirits whom God has sent to direct different lines of spiritual evolution." Furthermore, "it is undeniable that the organized spiritualist does not accept vicarious atonement or original sin." As for those texts of Scripture which teach the divinity of Christ, atonement, and original sin, Doyle cavalierly sweeps them away with the facile remark, "The New Testament has been doctored again and again in order to square the record of the Scriptures with the practice of the Church."

And he makes his profession of faith—and of unfaith: "Personally, I accept the view of the organized Spiritual religion, for it removes the difficulties which formerly stood between me and the whole Christian system."

So, Spiritualism, with its dark rooms, its knocks and table-tipping, its banjos and phosphorescent faces, its graphophone selections and its vociferous "Nearer My God to Thee," smothering the sound of the creaking machinery, its multitudinous charlatans, picking the pockets and harrowing the hearts of bereaved worshipers who gather in the hope of receiving a message from dear departed relatives,—all this humbug "removes the difficulties" of the Christian Faith! How truly has Pascal said "*O vous incrédules, les plus crédules!*"

There is an old story of a Frenchman who had lost his Catholic Faith, and was asked by an Evangelistic woman, "Which of the sects have you joined?" He answered, "Madame, I confess that I have lost my faith, but I have not yet lost my reason." Poor Doyle has lost everything. He cannot believe Jesus Christ, but he can believe Bailey. He cannot believe the Bible, but he can believe that angels sing "Onward Christian

Soldiers" in the nursery. He attacks those who "doctored" the New Testament, but he defends those who are proved liars at a séance. He cannot accept the teaching of the infallible Church, but he believes a battalion of spiritualists who swear that they have seen the dead, face to face. A score of times in one volume, perhaps a thousand times on the platform, he has roundly berated bishops and priests and ministers, and has recorded vulgar and stupid stories of Chinese mediums who ridicule belief in the redemption through Jesus Christ, yet he complains bitterly of the narrow-mindedness of ministers who retaliate and declare that his lectures are responsible for a great increase of superstition amongst simple people. Yet, as far as we Catholics are concerned, there is in our hearts more pity than indignation for Conan Doyle. The harm that he is doing to others probably can never be undone. But we pray that God may take pity on him because of his simplicity, show him that he is being deceived and exploited by charlatans, and bring him back to the Faith of his fathers.

FRIEDRICH NIETZSCHE

I

Nietzsche is surely exhibit A for psychoanalysis. In that science he might well occupy the place held by "the Jukes" in sociology, and by "Typhoid Mary" amongst the medicos. If he could be considered as a type, and not as a "sport" (in the biological sense), he would be almost sufficient in himself to justify Freud. His father was a clergyman; his two grandfathers were clergymen; his uncles and great-uncles were clergymen; and therefore (Freud would say "therefore") *he* was a rampant and flamboyant atheist! The "suppressed urges" could no longer be suppressed.

Also, he was a perpetual invalid. He suffered constantly from headache; his eyesight was extremely defective; his stomach was weak; all exertion was anguish to him; he was a victim of narcotics; and he was cursed with insomnia. Therefore (again the Freudian "therefore") he apotheosized health, idolized brute strength, and personified physical power in the *Raubthier*, the "Blond Beast."

With his conscious mind, he rejected Darwinism, but in the unconscious, he was fascinated and obsessed by Darwin's notions of the "struggle for existence" and the "survival of the fittest." His "Blond Beast" is only the logical culmination of those discredited features of the Darwinian hypothesis.

Sometimes, however, Nietzsche's inhibitions produced direct, rather than reflex, results. Prevented by his infirmities from enjoying society, he hated human intercourse. Huneker says "he fled into exile to escape what Poe has called 'the tyranny of the human face.'"

Being shut off from the usual pleasures of men, he railed against the *bourgeois* enjoyments, "Wine, Woman, and Song." Indeed, finding life altogether hateful, he maliciously reviled those who could discover even a moment of joy among its disappointments and illusions. In fine, he was a pessimist, compared with whom Schopenhauer was only a *dilettante*. He would, perhaps, have favored Schopenhauer's project of one grand act of simultaneous universal suicide, as the only feasible means of obliterating the human race, but, he was perverse enough to consider mankind too base to be worthy of that happy ending. As for himself, he preferred to live and complain, rather than die and be silent.

Curiously enough, he was anti-patriotic. His *bête noire* was *Deutschland über Alles*. He left Germany, and lived by preference in Italy, partly, no doubt, because of his health, but chiefly because he despised his fellow Germans. Yet—such is the irony of fate—he is regarded as the philosopher, *par excellence*, of German patriotism. His teaching pervaded the schools and helped to produce such apostles of nationalism and *Schrecklichkeit* as Ludendorff, Hindenburg, and Von Tirpitz.

Finally he went mad. But he was, and still remains, after death, an amazingly influential madman. His fame has reached all the continents; his works have been translated into a dozen languages; his ideas have been expounded *ad infinitum.* Schools have sprung up, and schisms have arisen, over his doctrines. His disciples have fought furious battles in his name, against non-Nietzscheans and against one another. Outside of Germany his chief apostle and intellectual godchild is George Bernard Shaw, who credits Nietzsche as his only master. A multitude of others, less frank than Shaw, are nevertheless actively disseminating Nietzscheanism. Indeed, it may be said with truth that those who are anti-Christian, those who ridicule or ignore the philosophy of the Sermon on the Mount, and those who believe that Christianity cannot be put into practice between nation and nation (or perhaps even between man and man), are all more Nietzschean than they imagine or admit.

II

The most typical work of Nietzsche is *Zarathustra.*[1] Zarathustra (a variant spelling of Zoroaster), is sometimes Nietzsche himself, sometimes a god, and sometimes the Superman—the Blond Beast.

The book is written in the sententious and dithyrambic style of the Psalms or Proverbs. It apes the solemnity of Sacred Scripture. Nietzsche claims that he wrote it in an ecstatic mood, and, as it were, under inspiration. Its purpose is to destroy morality. Nietzsche considers Zarathustra the creator of "that most portentous error, morality," and thinks that the same god (or prophet) should be the first to recognize his mistake.

[1] *Also Sprach Zarathustra.*

"Through me," says Nietzsche, "will come the destruction of morality. I am the first Immoralist." He attacks morality, not as a hedonist, but as a philosopher. He rejects human responsibility, guilt, and sin. He teaches that man is a mere tool of necessity. All ethical codes and commandments are "*Sklaven-moral*," slave morality, fit only for the common horde. Men of higher nature, and especially supermen, cannot sin and need no law. They are a law unto themselves. They create their own ethics. The superman does as he pleases, and whatever he does is right.

Some Christian writers, curiously sympathetic with Nietzsche, after explaining that he is easily misunderstood, have attempted to read into his attack upon morality a plea for a higher morality than that of law. Or they say that Nietzsche's idea is merely that "laws too high for the moral level of mankind are as bad as laws too low," and that "our ethical system must be accomodated to our capacity, and consequently must be made by ourselves."

Now, of course, it is possible, if one be so disposed, to interpret Nietzsche's idea in a noble sense. One may even compare his doctrine, "*Think*, and then do as you like," with St. Augustine's "*Love*, and do as you like," or even with St. John's "He that loveth cannot sin." But, unfortunately, one who is bent upon giving so flattering an interpretation of Nietzsche's gospel of immoralism, is confronted with his reiterated blasphemies against Christ and the Gospel. If Nietzsche understood himself, he was the antithesis of Christ. He intended his philosophy to be that of Antichrist.

A Christian, therefore, who persists in putting a high and holy meaning on Nietzsche's phrases, may be commended for his charity, rather than for his judgment. Any attempt to make immoralism moral can result only in a *tour de force*.

The Nietzschean view of morality is specifically illustrated by his famous division of morality into two kinds, "Slave Morality" and "Master Morality" ("*Sklavenmoral*" and "*Herrenmoral*"). The "Slave," that is, the ordinary man of no genius, must abide by rules and laws and commandments, which are the embodiment of the principles of "good" and "right." But the "master," the man of genius or of power, is "beyond good and evil"; he is self-sufficing; he is not subject to any established rule of moral values. He makes his own values. Whatever he does is right, not because he is too high-minded to do wrong, but because wrong is right if he does it. Strong men, talented men, men of outstanding power,—either intellectual or physical power,—are immune to the judgments of lesser men. Again and again Nietzsche declares that "we savants" are beyond good and evil.

Intellectually, Nietzsche is an ultra-aristocrat. To him democracy is contemptible. The elevation of the masses is impossible, and indeed undesirable. So far apart are the classes, or the "castes," of human society, that the laws of morality that apply to one are an insult and an affront to the other.

There are persons—not only Nietzscheans, but Christians—who virtually accept the idea that men of genius are "beyond good and evil." Not only do they make allowance for what is generally called "the artistic temperament," in judging men's lapses from morality, but they say, "Surely you are not going to judge a man of genius by the same standard as a day laborer." The Christian answers that a man of higher talent and better opportunities should be judged more rigorously than the man of poorer parts and lesser opportunities. But the Nietzschean believes that an artist, or a poet, a prima donna, a great tenor, a statesman, or a genius of any sort, a Sarah Bernhardt, a George Eliot, a Shelley, a Byron, a Napoleon, a Rockefeller, a Morgan, a Stinnes, is permitted to break the laws of morality and go, not only unpunished, but unrebuked.

As for individuals, so for nations. In the Nietzschean system, a powerful nation has no moral responsibility. The Blond Beast smashes his way through all human conventions and all moral codes. To the superman—and the superstate—a treaty is a scrap of paper; a contract is binding only on the weaker party; and even the Ten Commandments have no more binding force than the Code of Hammurabi. There has been much questioning, in recent years, as to "what's wrong with the world." Here, at least, is one thing wrong: supermen, supercorporations, supergovernments, considering themselves "beyond good and evil," immune to criticism, and independent of moral codes.

Let us not flatter ourselves with the fancy that Nietzsche's immoralism is found exclusively in one nation, the nation that gave him birth. His ideas have been acclimated north and south, and on all continents. Roughly speaking, all diplomacy is Nietz-schean. A large percentage of "patriotism" is pure Nietzscheanism. A newspaper (claiming to be the greatest in America) carried daily at the head of its editorial page, during the war, the motto, "My country! May she always be right. But right or wrong, my country!" That is the essence of Nietzschean im-moralism. An imperial power may cruelly abuse a colony—near enough and weak enough to be quickly reached and swiftly punished; that, too, is Nietz-scheanism. When international disputes arise between a great nation and a small people, the greater "bull-dozes" the smaller. That is Nietzscheanism. "The Blond Beast has no altruistic considerations, and we can hardly conceive of an orderly universe in which the owl should give himself up to the service of the mouse, and the lion lay down his life for the lamb. The old system of valuing extolled only the qualities favorable to the weak, suffering, and 'modern' race; so the new and reversed system of valuing ought to rear a healthy, a strong, lively, and courageous type." [1] "A few strong men are worth all the rest of the world. They *are* the world, the only world that deserves to be reckoned with. The weak and the unworthy should learn self-sacrifice, and leave the practice of self-assertion to the Superman." [2]

So far was Nietzsche influenced by the theory of evolution that he applied it to explain the existence

[1] *Zarathustra*, Introduction, p. 11.
[2] Nietzsche's views as interpreted by M. Petre, in *The Catholic World*, June, 1906, p. 351.

of the superman. As man is evolved from the brute, so the superman shall be evolved from man. What the evolutionists call *homo sapiens*, he prefers to call, contemptuously, *moral man*, and explains that one of the consequences (or perhaps not a consequence but a cause) of man's evolution from the beast is that man developed a moral sense. He must again lose that moral sense before he can evolve into superman. The superman is therefore in some respects an advance upon *homo sapiens* and yet also a reversion to the brute. In spite of his intellectual superiority, the superman will be more brutish than moral man. He will have the instinctive lawlessness of the brute, together with the conscious and voluntary lawlessness of the supra-moral man. It is an illuminating commentary upon this doctrine that Nietzsche's own nation, a decade after his death, came to be regarded as the intellectual leader of the world, and at the same time the principal advocate of brute-force—probably the most paradoxical phenomenon in all our self-contradictory civilization.

During the war, we saw exemplified the doctrine of the supernation. Since the war we have seen again the advent of something akin to the superman—the dictator who takes possession of a tottering state, rules it by main strength, asserting the principle that might is right and that the end justifies the means. Democratic principles and democratic institutions are, temporarily at least, in abeyance. Parliaments and kings automatically do what dictators command. If a Napoleon Bonaparte had appeared a year or two ago, in the midst of the political and financial disorders that followed the Great War, as one appeared during the chaos that ensued upon the French Revolution, he might have taken over all the Mediterranean countries under one dictatorship and then have subjugated the remainder of Europe.

Doubtless, the democratic instinct will reassert itself in our days. At least it will do so if the nations that call themselves republics or democracies do not further play into the hands of dictators by selfishly prolonging chaotic conditions. But it would be more to the mind of Nietzsche if a Napoleon, or a Charlemagne, or a Frederick Hohenstaufen should arise and absolutely dominate the European scene. If mountains of corpses were to be piled up, and rivers of blood to flow, it would not matter to Nietzche, provided that the rule of the superman were to be assured.

III

So far the Nietzschean idea of political autocracy. But Nietzsche is even more fervently devoted to the idea of an intellectual autocracy. He goes so far as to regret the passing of the institution of slavery, because— as he explains—the superman can be free for intellectual pursuits only on condition that multitudes of helots, or serfs, shall relieve the intellectual aristocracy from all attention to menial matters. "When slavery was abolished," he says, "the fairest fruits of culture were lost and can never flourish again." It is his notion that Socrates and Plato were made possible by the Greek system of slavery, just as the building of the pyramids was made possible by the existence of multitudes of *fellahin*, whose lives were of no account, who might be driven to death, and who had neither the right nor the power to make an effective protest against the cruelty of the system that crushed them. Others than Nietzsche have blamed Christianity because it did not immediately extirpate slavery, and introduce industrial freedom. Nietzsche blames Christianity because it did extirpate slavery. It reminds one of the well-known chapter, "The Paradoxes of Christianity," in Chesterton's *Orthodoxy*, in which he shows with his usual skill and humor, the contradictory charges made against the Christian religion. It was too meek and too haughty, too peaceful and too warlike, too sheepish and too cruel. So Christianity is blamed for abolishing slavery and for not abolishing slavery.

There is one feature of Nietzsche's doctrine of the superman which seems (at least when examined in the light of mere reason, apart from the supernatural standard of Christian virtue) to be quite defensible. He protests against the sapping of the strength of the superman, by blood-sucking, neurasthenic, neurotic, hysterical people, or by mere weaklings. There are parasitic persons whose very presence has a tendency to devitalize the strong, and whose insistent and petulant demands for assistance, care, and comfort wear down the patience and dissipate the strength of men whose powers should be conserved for the doing of some great work. Even Jesus was constrained to say, "I feel that power has gone out of Me." He, indeed, had an inexhaustible fund of spiritual strength. He could afford to give prodigally. But not every man can stand heavy and continuous draught upon his mental and spiritual store. The strength of men can be drained dry by the vampire-like demands of mental and moral weaklings.

The true Christian, when called upon to give not only of his mind and heart, but of himself, will doubtless aim to be as prodigally generous as Christ. He will say, with St. Paul, that he is "willing to spend and be spent." But the natural man will be more inclined to cry, "Deliver me from my importunate and dependent friends!" Particularly will he feel that he has a just cause of grievance, if he be compelled to minister of his intellectual and emotional resources, to those who seem not to be made stronger by the communication of his strength; who remain empty after they have been filled, and weak after power has been imparted to them.

Nietzsche's doctrine is that such sacrifices as these, on the part of the great, should be made unnecessary and impossible. He would treasure and develop the strength of the strong. He would let the weaklings die. He would forbid the healthy to endanger themselves by waiting upon the sick. He would segregate the stupid, and leave the lame and the halt behind in the march of human progress. "The weak and the unsuccessful shall perish," he cries, "and we will even help them to perish. . . . This is our love of mankind." [1] In a word, his philosophy is the antithesis both of Christianity and of democracy. There could be no better demonstration of the fact that pa-

[1] *Antichrist*, p. 2.

ganism is, in the most offensive sense of the word, "aristocratic," and that democracy is a purely Christian product.

The plea to be delivered from the demands of one's dependents is, furthermore, a confession of weakness. Those who complain that they are irritated by neurasthenics beyond all possibility of self-control, are, to a degree, neurasthenic themselves. If one protests that he has just so much spiritual reserve, and no more, and that consequently he cannot afford to be doling out his strength to every beggar that makes a plea to him, he has, of course, no right to call himself a superman. But after all there was only one Superman in human history, Who could give and lose nothing; Who could spend Himself and yet not be spent. It is a profound pity that poor, mad Nietzsche had not the spiritual discernment to recognize the superman in Christ, rather than in Anti-Christ.

Nietzsche himself was so far from possessing an inexhaustible spiritual vitality, that he could not tolerate even the patient and loving ministrations of his sister, who was as self-sacrificing in her devotion to him as Henriette was to Renan. "His sister," says Huneker, "who nursed him from his breakdown in 1888 till his death in 1900, and who for twenty years made such a successful propaganda for his ideas, was, in the last three letters, grievously insulted by her brother."[1] He called her a "meddlesome woman," who "did not understand his ideas." He declared that she "martyred" him, and "made him ridiculous." Yet it is

[1] Huneker, *Egoists: A Book of Supermen*, p. 259.

scarcely beyond the truth to say that without her constant patient nursing he could not have lived, and without her zealous propaganda, his writings would have
been ignored. Those who have had experience with
petulant and unappreciative invalids will understand
that Nietzsche, and not his sister, was the weakling.
Judged by the Christian standard, her life was
nobler than his. She gave of her strength, and he received. Yet with the typical ingratitude and soul-
blindness of a megalomaniac, he imagined himself the
Superman and complained that she exhausted him!
He further exposes his weakness when he writes, "This
is what my love for the distant demands of me, to have
no care for the nearest." Here again he might have
learned a lesson from Christ, Who loved all mankind
with a passionate fervor unequaled in human history,
and yet had the tenderest affection for those who were
His daily companions and His intimates. Again I say,
it is pitiable in Nietzsche not to have been able to recognize the true Superman. On the contrary, he is always
particularly violent when he speaks of Jesus. He calls
Him "that immodest one, the singular saint and advocate of petty people, who testified 'I am the truth.'
Thou, O Zarathustra passedst him by and saidst, 'Nay,
nay, three times nay!'"[1] With a momentary forgetfulness of the fact that he is sworn to show no pity, he
even seems to commiserate with the followers of Christ.
He cries, "O that someone would save them from their
Savior." [2]

[1] *Zarathustra*, p. 266.
[2] *Ibid.*, p. 103.

We Catholics are, and have been for many centuries, accustomed to obscene and vicious denunciations of the Church and the Pope. But generally the anti-Catholic fanatics, while denouncing the Church and the Vicar of Christ, pretend to love Christ. Not so with Nietzsche. He will be no mealy-mouthed hypocrite. His only virtue seems to have been a consistent hatred of hypocrisy. He could not abide the cowardice of those who gave up belief in Christ but had not the courage to reject the moral system of Christ. He himself damns Christianity, root and branch, Master and disciples. "Rome hath turned harlot," he cries, "Rome's Cæsar a beast, and God hath turned Jew."[1]

IV

Of all Christian doctrines, Nietzsche particularly detested that of the Cross as a means of sanctification and salvation. Or if there could be any other feature of Christianity which he equally despised, it was that of pity and mercy. Therefore, probably nothing that we could say would make him so frantic as that we *pity* him because he did not grasp the significance of the Gospel of the Cross. If any man needed that Gospel, it was he. He was in constant pain, physical and mental. Suffering made him bitter and finally drove him crazy. The philosophy of resignation, of peaceful and willing suffering as a means of purification of soul, might have saved his reason. But he fought the Cross and became stark mad.

In his madness, he continued to be obsessed with the

[1] *Zarathustra*, p. 248.

thought of the Cross which he had so furiously rejected. He called his autobiography *Ecce Homo.* He signed his letters, "The Crucified One," and as a constantly recurring refrain in his writings he says, "God is dead." In a moment of illumination, he penned his most famous saying, "The only Christian died on the Cross." Huneker answers that gibe with a retort, equally cruel, though not equally clever, "The only Nietzschean went mad when Nietzsche's brain crumbled." Others, more introspective than Huneker, will make no attempt to answer that scathing sentence of Nietzsche with a smart saying, but will take it with them into their meditations. Caiaphas spoke one true prophetic sentence. Why not Nietzsche? "The only Christian died on the Cross!" It is dangerously close to the truth.

V

I am not directly concerned, in a discourse on Nietzsche, with the Divinity of Christ, but as a corollary to the poor mad philosopher's insensate hatred of Christianity, I may permit myself a moment to say that the Personality of Jesus Christ has infinite power to absorb the attention even of those who compel themselves to fight against Him. One may love Christ or hate Him, but one cannot ignore Him. It is possible to hate Buddhism or Mohammedanism, but no one hates Buddha or Mohammed. Also no one loves Buddha or Mohammed. Similarly we may have a mild interest in Socrates, with perhaps a gently affectionate regard for him, but we do not love Socrates. Neither does any one hate Socrates; nobody furiously denounces him; nobody curses him. But Christ is different. Unlike Socrates and Buddha and Mohammed, He may be loved without limit, or hated without stint, but He cannot be merely tolerated or patronized. Those who profess to be indifferent to Christ, and—I may add—those who profess to be indifferent to His Church, have not deeply considered either Christ or His Church.

As for poor Nietzsche, he was, for the last ten or twelve years of his life, insane. But before his mind failed, and even afterwards, in the ravings which were only the automatic continuation of the ideas of his less insane years, he recognized the fact that indifference, mental, moral, religious, is cowardice. At least he was consistent. He saw that faith and morals stand or fall together. He was mad but not blind. He knew that to attempt to maintain Christian morality while rejecting Christian faith is a type of madness less evident and less spectacular than his own, but madness none the less. If one will be pagan, one must be thoroughly pagan, one cannot be Christiano-pagan or pagano-Christian. If the modern world learns that simple fact, the modern world will be saved.

Furthermore, it would be a mark of sanity for us to recognize another fact that the crazy man saw clearly: to attempt to maintain society on pagan principles, while individuals within that society live on Christian principles, is sheer lunacy. Perhaps, after all, the madman was no madder than our contemporary diplomats, who are trying to persuade us to live nationally and internationally as pagans, but to live individually as Christians. If we can learn wisdom out of the mouths of babes, may we not learn sanity out of the mouth of a madman? In any event, let us render to Nietzsche the tribute that he would least appreciate but that we know to be best, the tribute of our sympathy and pity. He can do us no harm, for he expresses his anti-Christian principles so honestly that we instinctively shrink from them as we instinctively cling to Christ.

ERNST HAECKEL

I

It is odd that a man like Charles Darwin should have for champion a man like Ernst Haeckel. No two men could be more opposite in character. Darwin was diffident about himself and about his doctrine; Haeckel was arrogantly certain. Darwin knew his limitations; he made few if any incursions into the foreign field of philosophy. Haeckel, not content with his reputation as a scientist, persistently encroached upon the ground of philosophy and of theology. Darwin said, humbly enough, that though he might claim to know something about the origin of species, he knew nothing about the origin of life. Haeckel claimed to know the solution of the riddle of life—and of all the other world-riddles. Darwin loved seclusion; Haeckel was over-fond of the limelight. Darwin was deferential to the opinions of others; Haeckel was truculent toward those who disagreed with him. Darwin sought peace; Haeckel reveled in controversy. In the few recorded utterances of Darwin about theology, he seems to speak with regret, and even with pathos, of his inability to profess the Christian faith. Haeckel, on the contrary, was an exultant atheist, and took malicious delight in loud-mouthed blasphemy. In fine, Darwin was always the scientist; Haeckel was sometimes a scientist, but frequently a demogogue and dogmatist.

Consequently, men of science have almost universally

expressed disgust with Haeckel. Professor His said of him, "He has forfeited, through his methods of fighting, the right to be counted an equal in the company of serious investigators." Dr. Dwight [1] records that Agassiz's tone in dealing with Haeckel was "not that of one arguing with an equal, but of one exposing a knave." Dwight himself says, "The hero (Haeckel) is but a quack." Alfred Russel Wallace, codiscoverer with Darwin of the theory of natural selection, says, "I have no sympathy with Haeckel's unfounded dogmatism of combined negation and omniscience, more especially when the assumption of superior knowledge seems to be put forward to conceal his real ignorance of the nature of life itself." [2]

But if Haeckel is recognized by scientists as something of a charlatan, he is held by the mass of believers in evolution to be something of a prophet. He is incomparably more "popular" than Darwin. Probably for every one reader of Darwin's difficult and painstaking *Origin of Species*, there are fifty thousand readers of Haeckel's fascinating—and fallacious—*The Riddle of the Universe*. Indeed, that volume is one of the world's "best sellers." It has been translated into a score of languages, and its sale has run to millions of copies. Not only in Germany, therefore, but in all the world, Haeckel and not Darwin is the popular apostle of "Darwinism." True, Haeckel's Darwinism varies greatly from Darwin's Darwinism, but Haeckel's

[1] *Thoughts of a Catholic Anatomist.* By Thomas A. Dwight, M. D., Parkman Professor of Anatomy, Harvard, 1883–1911. Longmans, N. Y., 1912.
[2] *The World of Life*, p. 7.

is the brand that is known to the multitude. Speaking broadly, when the man in the street mentions "evolution" he has Haeckelism, not Darwinism, in mind. Semi-educated men, who form the bulk of our population,—and of every population,—are not interested in minutely reasoned biological or anthropological treatises, but they are captivated by sensational philosophical and theological theories such as those of Haeckel. They have not the capacity for following a rigidly scientific discussion. But they are easily interested and beguiled by a man who, in the name of science, declares that "evolution" has done away with God, free will, and moral responsibility.

Man is naturally religious, that is, he is instinctively interested in religion,—whether he be for it or against it,—but his interest in "science" must be artificially produced and generally remains superficial. Men are interested in evolution, not because of its scientific importance, but because of its religious importance. Generally speaking, they have neither the patience nor the ability to follow Darwin's meticulously laborious reasonings from observed phenomena; they know only his principal thesis, and that none too accurately. But Darwin's phrases, "the struggle for existence," and "the survival of the fittest," make an appeal to the imagination—and fascinate the unscholarly. "Evolution" to the ordinary man means, not the origin of species by natural selection, but the development of man from the monkey!

Hence the wide popularity of such a book as Haeckel's *The Riddle of the Universe*. That title itself captivated the fancy of the ordinary reader. The volume, in substance, had been published under the title *General Morphology*, but the public whom Haeckel sought to interest didn't even know the meaning of the word "morphology." So he adroitly revised the work, popularized it, made it spectacular, rhetorical, sensational, gave it the catchy title, achieved a prodigious popular success, and garnered enormous royalties. But in so doing, he sacrificed much of his reputation as a scientist. Stepping out of his character to play the part of a propagandist of infidelity, he became, not only obnoxious to religious-minded people, but ridiculous and hateful in the eyes of his fellow scientists.

II

Ernst Haeckel was born in Potsdam, Prussia in 1834. He was, therefore, a young man in 1859, when Darwin's revolutionary treatise appeared. Immediately he became an enthusiastic Darwinian. Gradually he developed a mania against religion. He seems to have considered himself possessed of two vocations—the one, research in the fields of biology and zoölogy; the other, controversy in the realm of theology. It is always risky for a scholar to step out of his own province. Darwin was aware of that danger. His Christian faith had slowly slipped away from him. He became, however, not a militant atheist, but a "gentle skeptic." And he declared his opinion that "a man ought not to publish on a subject to which he has not given special and continuous thought." He might have said, with equal justice, that a man ought not to publish on a subject unless it be his life's work.

Men of science, tempted to think themselves philosophers, need above all men to be reminded of the homely maxim, "Shoemaker, stick to your last." When, for example, Thomas A. Edison is in his laboratory, experimenting with electricity, he is the incomparable "wizard." When he stops for a few minutes to grant an interview for a Sunday newspaper, on the immortality of the soul, he is rash and becomes ridiculous. Likewise, when Mr. Henry Ford prophesies that he will turn out of his factory a "flivver a minute," we say, "How wonderful!" When he says that he "would not give a nickel for all the art in the galleries of Europe," we say, "How asinine!" It is said that Edison spends eighteen hours a day in his workshop. That—together with his genius—is why he is a great inventor. It is also the reason why he is not, and cannot be, a theologian. One who spends three-quarters of every twenty-four hours in one kind of study has no time for another study. Philosophy and theology (contrary to the common view) do not come to a man by instinct or inspiration, but by labor and the expenditure of time. Consequently, the opinion of an electrical engineer on immortality is no better than the opinion of a blacksmith, and probably not so good as the opinion of a cobbler. Mr. Edison should cling close to his dynamos and eschew theology.

So of Mr. Ford: he is a good tinsmith, but no one who sees the product of his factory would consider him an artist. A sign-painter, or a sand-sculptor, is a better

judge of art. Indeed, the poorest and raggedest son
of little Italy knows more than Mr. Ford about Rubens
and Titian and Michelangelo. The uneducated and
uncultured manufacturer would be wiser if he knew his
limitations.

Ernst Haeckel is no exception to the rule. He knows
much about Radiolaria, and Siphonophora, and deep-
sea Ceratosa, but he is not thereby entitled to speak
with authority on the Trinity, the Incarnation, and the
Immortality of the Soul. Science deals with facts and
phenomena, or at the most with secondary causes; it
has nothing authentic to say about the First Cause. It
deals with matter; spirit is beyond its ken.

Curiously, however, there are multitudes of persons
who prefer to take their theology from almost any one
rather than a theologian, as there are multitudes who
take medicine recommended by a chauffeur, or a brick-
layer, rather than by a doctor. Still more curiously,
there are great numbers of those who love to be told
that there is no God and no soul; that human life is
only animal life, and human love only animal passion.
Even if these calamitous statements were true, it would
seem decent to communicate them reluctantly and to
receive them with disappointment. But the apostles of
materialism and "scientific" atheism seem to take a
wild delight in their unholy vocation of ruining the
ideals and aspirations of mankind. And the recipients
of the melancholy evangel of despair are unwarrantably
and incomprehensibly gleeful over the news that their
ancestors were anthropoid apes, and that they themselves are only highly organized beasts. With an air

of triumph as if he were proclaiming the news of the Resurrection, Haeckel cries out, "Man who exalted himself to the heavens, man who claimed to be the off-spring of gods, and demigods, is found to be only a 'placental mammal,' of no more value in the scheme of things than the microscopic Infusoria." And for these inspiring words he is rated as the prophet of a new and better dispensation.

Surely it is one of the most curious of all psychological phenomena that man should rejoice at having a pair of beasts rather than a man and woman for his first parents. A man will furiously resent what has been called "the imputation of canine maternity." But the same man will consider with equanimity, and accept without proof, the statement that his ancestors were apes.

Man on occasion, seems glad to be rid of his dignity. "Who steals my purse, steals trash," says the poet; "but he that filches from me my good name, robs me of that which not enriches him, and leaves me poor indeed." But when Haeckel, in the most high-handed manner, robs man of his good name and tells him that he is of no more value to the universe than bugs which live in a puddle of mud and die in a day, man strangely swells with pride and satisfaction. Just so, there are men who, revolting from the doctrine of the divine dignity of the human race, love to be told that we are only ants and that this planet is only an ant-hill in the infinite cosmos.

Not content with debasing man, Haeckel insults God with the utterance, "God is only a gaseous vertebrate."

Millions of men read the coarse blasphemy, not only without indignation, but apparently with pleasure and satisfaction. True scientists, like Professor Conklin of Princeton, protest against the grossness of such a statement, but apparently there are other scientists, and surely there are non-scientists, who welcome an insult to God as enthusiastically as an insult to the human race.

III

However, these crimes against God and man are of lesser importance, in the eyes of scientists, than Haeckel's deliberate "scientific" falsifications. Here we come upon one of the most surprising and dis-edifying facts in all the history of modern science. In a lecture at Jena, on "The Problem of Man," Haeckel drew skeletons of a man, a gorilla, a chimpanzee, an orang-outang, and a gibbon. Wherever dissimilarities occurred he minimized them; similarities he magnified. Also, he drew a human head upon the embryo of an ape. Likewise, in his *Natural History of Creation*, he printed three cuts, representing the ova of a man, a monkey and a dog, and three other cuts representing the embryos of a dog, a fowl, and a tortoise. He then pointed out that in no instance could a difference be found between one and another of the ova, or of the embryos. But Professor Rutimeyer of Basel discovered that Haeckel had in each case merely printed the same cut three times, and called the pictures, in one instance, man, monkey, dog, and, in the other, dog, fowl, tortoise. When the diagrams were published,

Dr. Brass accused Haeckel of fraud. "Not only," he said, "has Professor Haeckel falsely represented the various evolutionistic changes of man, the monkey, and other mammifers, but he has even taken from the work of a scientist the figure of a macaco, cut off its tail, and made a gibbon of it."

Thereupon commenced a controversy as acrimonious as any sixteenth-century theological debate. Haeckel's most telling retort was by epithets and doubtless the most insulting of all his epithets (in his own mind and in that of his adversary) was when he called Dr. Brass a "Protestant Jesuit."

Not content with falsification, he perpetrated downright falsehood. He wrote: "In the last twenty years a considerable number of well-preserved fossil skeletons of anthropoid and other apes have been discovered, and amongst them are all the important intermediate forms which constitute a series of ancestors connecting the oldest anthropoid ape with man." If this were true, the "missing link" would be no longer missing. But Alfred Russel Wallace was writing, at about the same time, "There is not merely one missing link, but at least a score of them" and Father Muckermann declares, "Haeckel's curious 'Progonotaxis,' or genealogy of man, is pure fiction. It consists of thirty stages, beginning with the 'moners' and ending with *homo loquax*. The *first fifteen stages have no fossil representatives*." [1]

Perhaps even more startling then Haeckel's dishonesty in fabricating drawings, is the fact that he ulti-

[1] *Catholic Encyclopedia*, Art. "Evolution."

mately admitted the fraud. He confessed: "Six or eight per cent of my drawings of embryos are really falsified. We are obliged to fill the vacancies with hypotheses." But immediately he declared, in his own defense, that it is customary for scientists to make use of fraudulent designs. "I have the satisfaction," he says, "of knowing that side by side with me in the prisoner's dock, stand hundreds of fellow culprits, many of them among the most esteemed biologists. The majority of figures, morphological, anatomical, histological, which are circulated and valued in students' manuals, and in reviews and works of biology deserve in the same degree the charge of being falsified. None of them is exact. All of them are more or less adapted, schematized, reconstructed."

This is interesting, if true. Obviously we cannot consider it true on Haeckel's authority. A liar will lie about men as well as about embryos. But, on the other hand, a liar sometimes tells the truth. A criminal, undergoing the "third degree," will lie, and continue to lie for hours or even for days. But if he is suddenly cornered and admits one lie, it is a well-recognized psychological fact that he will probably break down and tell all the truth he knows. Indeed, he may tell so many true things as not only to incriminate his companions, but to embarrass his investigators. I suspect that it is so in Haeckel's case. Angered at being caught in a fraud, he "peaches" on his fellow scientists. He admits the lie, and then proceeds to "spill the beans."

Indeed, there is not a little deception among scientists about the larger question of the certainty attached to the hypothesis of evolution. So reliable and careful an authority as Dr. Dwight says: "Very few of the leaders of science dare to tell the truth concerning the state of their mind. They would not tell an untruth, yet they write and speak as if evolution were an absolute certainty as well-established as the law of gravitation." And he accuses some of them of "cringing to public opinion." The theory of evolution has won its place in the universities. Hardly any one in the world of learning dares to oppose it or even seriously to criticize it. Dr. Thomas Hunt Morgan of Princeton says: "Biologists have many doubts which they do not publish. The claims of the opponents that Darwinism has become a dogma contains more truth than the nominal follower of the schools finds pleasant to hear." [1]

The entire subject of fraud in natural science, especially in connection with the theory of evolution, is so important—so much more important than Haeckel—that it may be well to digress for a moment or two, and call attention to the fact that there has been a vast amount either of conscious deceit, or of unconscious but blameworthy misrepresentation, amongst biologists, anatomists, and anthropologists overeager to convince the public of the truth of evolution. Even Huxley is not blameless in this matter. In his well-known summary of the evolution of the horse, he records the steps of the progress as follows: "First, there is the true horse, as we now know him. Next we have the American Pliocene form, Pliohippus. Then comes Protohippus, having one large toe and two small ones

[1] Quoted in Dwight, *Thoughts of a Catholic Anatomist*, p. 43.

on each foot. Next, Miohippus, with three complete toes. Then the older Miocene Mesohippus, with three toes in front and one large splint-like toe immediately behind. Last (most remote) we have Orohippus with four complete toes on the front feet and three toes on the hind feet." [1]

These are offered as the steps in the progress of the horse as discovered in America. It is disconcerting, therefore, to learn that "the true horse," the horse as we know him, was not found in America by the first white men, but was introduced from Europe, in the time of Columbus. The fossil remains found in America may perhaps be those of ancestors of the European horse, but the fact that the American horse was extinct is a detail not mentioned by Huxley.

Sir J. W. Dawson declares that the "existing American horses, which are of European origin, are descendants of Paleotherium, and not of Eohippus," and he brushes away Huxley's carefully constructed theory with the abrupt statement, "Such genealogies are not of the nature of scientific evidence." [2] That is to say, Huxley, like Haeckel, was drawing upon his imagination.

Apropos of the evolution of the horse, I am sure that Dr. James J. Walsh's humorous description of the process that is alleged to have taken place will be entertaining and instructive: "The little ancestor of the horse, about the size of the rabbit, or probably a little smaller to begin with, wanted to be bigger and to run

[1] Quoted in Dwight, *Thoughts of a Catholic Anatomist*, p. 43.
[2] Quoted in Gerard, *The Oldest Riddle and the Newest Answer*, p. 246.

faster. He wanted so much to run fast that he touched the ground in his eager haste only with the middle toe of each foot, and did this so constantly that gradually the other toes began to atrophy, and eventually disappeared. His anxiety to get larger made him lift himself up ever more and more, until, finally, he began to run on the toe nail of this middle toe, adding at least a part of a cubit to his stature, and this middle toe became a hoof. See how easy it is for the horse to create himself." [1]

Professor Henry Fairfield Osborn, I may add, has said, "It would not be true to say that the evolution of man rests upon evidence as complete as that of the evolution of the horse." Father LeBuffe quotes Bateson, Ranke, Virchow, Steinmann, and Vernon Kellogg in support of the statement that "the evolution of the horse is scarcely more than a very moderately supported hypothesis." You may draw your own conclusion about the certainty of the evolution of man.

Unfortunately the habit of "adapting, schematizing, and reconstructing,"—of calling upon the imagination to fill up the gaps in the record of evolution,—of drawing fanciful pictures of "missing links" that, of course, have never been seen,—is not confined to textbooks of biology. The newspapers have caught the habit. In particular, the screechingly sensational Sunday Supplements are addicted to pseudo-science.

In the New York Sunday *American* for August 7, 1921, there is an entire page of "faked" illustrations—

[1] Walsh, *The Comedy of Evolution*, in *The Catholic World*, October, 1922.

of men with tails like monkeys, with the legs, hands, and feet of monkeys, and with bodies entirely covered with monkey-like hair. The picture is described in an accompanying article, written by an alleged famous "scientist." To the ignorant readers of that sheet (their name is millions), the picture is proof sufficient of the truth of human evolution. Naturally, one does not expect the editors of a popular Sunday supplement to have scruples about scientific accuracy. But it is to the shame of science that sensation-mongers can claim to take their cue from scholars who know better. The bad example was set by Haeckel and Huxley. It is not strange that it should be followed by such as William Randolph Hearst.

IV

To return to Haeckel. I have contrasted him with Darwin, and have called him a dogmatist. Some painstaking student of Darwin (apparently having plenty of leisure) counted the phrase, "we may well suppose," over eight hundred times in Darwin's two chief works, *The Origin of Species* and *The Descent of Man*. But in Haeckel there is no such timidity of expression. His favorite phrases are: "It must have been," "it is impossible to doubt," "it is inconceivable," "we are compelled to assume," and the like.

To give just a sample or two of his scientific method. He is enumerating his famous thirty stages in the evolution of man, "fifteen of which have no fossil representatives." He says: "The vertebrate ancestor, number fifteen, akin to the salamanders, *must have been* a species of lizard. There remains to us *no fossil relic* of this animal. In no respect did he resemble any form actually existing. Nevertheless comparative anatomy and ontogeny authorize us in affirming that he once existed. We will call this animal Protamnion." This, be it remembered, is science, not poetry. But was there ever a better example of the poet's truth that "Imagination bodies forth the form of things unknown . . . turns them to shapes, and gives to airy nothing a local habitation and a name! "

Let us suppose that a Biblical historian were to argue thus: "In regard to the genealogy of Christ, we have decided *a priori* that from Joseph to King David there must have been twenty-eight generations. We have the record of the second fourteen generations from Joseph back to the transmigration of Babylon. The records of the first fourteen generations, from the transmigration of Babylon back to King David are missing. But our theory of twice fourteen authorizes us in affirming that there were fourteen from Jechonias to David, and we will name them Josiah, Ezechias, and so on." One can imagine with what contempt Haeckel would spew upon such calculations. But he, wishing to trace the genealogy of Homo sapiens back to the anthropoid ape, declares *a priori* that there were thirty stages, admits that the first fifteen are missing, but *assumes* them, and *names* them. And this is science.

It is, however, quite on a par with the procedure of every scientist who claims to be able to trace the genealogy of man back to the ape. As Alfred Russel Wallace says, in that genealogy there is, not one, but at least a score of "missing links." The unsophisticated layman, not knowing the use of hypothesis and imagination in biology, would imagine that "science" would refuse to *imagine* a stage in the process of which there is no evidence. Therein, of course, the layman would show his ignorance. Science builds upon imagination and hypothesis quite as much as the theologian builds upon faith. The natural sciences, like the mental sciences, are not halted by *lacunae*, or missing links. Indeed, if there were as many missing links in theology as there are in biology, no theologian would be bold enough to ask a hearing, and no theologian would expect anything but ridicule for his theories. But every evolutionist knows that you may ridicule theology because it does not prove its every step with mathematical precision. But you must not ridicule biology for making use of hypothesis. You must not even find fault with Haeckel when he "assumes" fifteen out of thirty links in the chain that binds man to the anthropoid ape.

Haeckel is not only dogmatically certain of evolution. He is dogmatically certain of monophyletic evolution; that is to say, he insists upon the theory that all animals and men have derived from one, and not several original species. With his customary cocksureness, he declares: "It is impossible to doubt that all reptiles, birds, and mammals had a common origin, and constitute a single main division of kindred forms. To this division belongs our race." [1] Again: "It is inconceivable that all existing and extinct mammals have sprung from several different and originally separate root forms. We are compelled, if we know anything, to assume (!) the monophyletic hypothesis. All animals, including man, must be traced from a single common mammalian parent form." [2] And he calls this an "irrefutable proposition."

So he dogmatizes against those of his fellow scientists who believe in evolution, though not monophyletic evolution, as truculently as against the imbeciles who will not believe in evolution at all.

Let us, however, comment no more on the blatant dogmatism of those two passages. Let us pause only for a moment to make sure that the significant phrase,

[1] *Evolution of Man,* Vol. II, p. 136.
[2] *Ibid,* p. 142.

"We are compelled to assume," does not go unnoticed. In our simplicity, we may have held that "science" was not compelled to assume anything, but was prepared to prove everything. We stand corrected—and chastened. And if, also in our guilelessness, we imagined that no one could be compelled to assume "the monophyletic hypothesis" or any other hypothesis—that there was only one thing a scientifically-minded person is compelled to assume—a fact,—again let us confess that we are duly castigated and corrected.

But, being compelled to assume, not only evolution, but evolution of all reptiles, birds, and mammals, including man, from *one* root form, we cannot but lament that this makes evolution even harder to accept than we had anticipated. For there are limits, after all, to the power of the human imagination. It is not so hard to imagine that a hawk or an eagle had the same ultimate ancestor. But it is hard to imagine that an eagle and a humming bird are from the one same primary species. It is not hard to imagine that a dog and a wolf are from one stock. But the imagination is strained a bit when called upon to picture one common ancestor of the dog and the cat. A shark and a wren, a camel and a Pomeranian poodle, an elephant and a canary, a rhinoceros and a dachshund, a hippopotamus and a butterfly, a kangaroo and a tree toad may all be descended, not from various original species, but from one and the same original pair of progenitors. But the theory staggers the imagination. Ask me to believe that the zebra, the donkey, and the horse had

a common ancestor, and I say, "Quite probably!"
Tell me that the race horse, the draft horse, and the
cab horse are brothers, and I can believe you. Tell
me even that the tiger and the pussy cat are of one
species, and I will smother my rebellious imagination
and believe. But when you fulminate the dogma
that a hen is only a degraded dinosaur, or that a cow
is a walrus that took to the land, you must pardon me
if my mind balks a little before it will submit. Scientific faith makes a greater demand upon me than
theological faith. Yet, of the score of millions who have
read all these things in Haeckel, millions seem to believe
him without a struggle. But we simple folk who are
not overly scientific cannot understand why people
who believe all that, should hold up their hands in
scandal and horror when we say that we believe in the
Trinity or the Incarnation, or in life after death. A
man who can accept the brain-dizzying dogmas of
Ernst Haeckel should see no difficulty in a few little
theological mysteries.

Haeckel, though an unbeliever, has a creed of his
own. "The Universe," he says, "is eternal, infinite,
and illimitable." The devout evolutionist answers
"Credo!" "It evolved from a vast nebula of infinitely
attentuated material revolving upon its own axis."
"Credo!" "Its substance fills infinite space." "Credo!"
"It is in eternal motion." "Credo!" "Its movement
is innate." "Credo!" "Every living cell has psychic
properties." "Credo!" "Every cell has volition."
"Credo!" "The development of the universe is a
monistic mechanical process." "Credo!" "In that

process we discover no aim or purpose whatever." "Credo! Amen!"

Since we Christians must choose between this creed and that of the Apostles, we prefer the Apostles' Creed—"I believe in God the Father Almighty, Creator of heaven and earth," and the rest. It is simpler, less arbitrary, more reasonable, easier to believe.

Haeckel, however, is not the only dogmatic evolutionist. When an international council of scientists met at Cambridge, Mass., in 1922, a committee presented, by way of preliminary to the proceedings, the dogma of evolution: "The council affirmed" (note the dogmatic tone) "That so far as the scientific evidence of the evolution of plants, animals, *and man* are concerned, there is no ground whatever for the assertion that these evidences constitute a 'mere guess.' No scientific generalization is more strongly supported by thoroughly tested evidences than is that of organic evolution. The *evidences in favor of the evolution of man are sufficient to convince every scientist of note in the world.*" Remember that this proclamation was made before the discussion, as if to intimidate any delegate who might feel inclined to cherish any little scientific skepticism about the certainty of the evidence for evolution. To all intents and purposes the declaration was a dogmatic formula. It might have been worded: "If any one shall say that organic evolution of plants, animals, and man is not a scientifically established fact, let him be anathema." Naturally the Biblical word "anathema" is avoided. But, in effect, a scientist who should say that evolution is still only a "shrewd guess" (or to speak more accurately an "hypothesis") is excommunicated from the body of the learned. He is no longer a member of the society of the "scientists of note in the world." "To doubt evolution," says Professor Marsh, "is to doubt science."

Now this may all be quite true. But we laymen would like to see it put just a little less dogmatically. We should be more highly edified by the religion of science if its popes and prelates would say—and mean it: "Nothing is ever definitely settled in science. Science is always open to new information. It is contrary to the scientific method to promulgate any doctrine or dogma." But, to tell the truth, it would ruin the reputation of any but the greatest scientist in the world if he now questioned evolution.[1] His name would be anathema-maranatha. Let not the scientists accuse theologians of intolerance.

Finally, since this discourse on Haeckel has led, logically enough, to the discussion of the offensive dogmatism of some scientists, let us Christians take warning and be on our guard against undue dogmatism and intolerance. The Catholic Church has not issued any dogmatic definition upon the question of evolution. Catholic scientists are free to accept it or reject it.[2] Members of the Catholic Church ought not to usurp

[1] It is worthy of note that the illustrious Virchow, anatomist, archæologist, anthropologist and founder of the science of cellular pathology, objected to the teaching of evolution in the schools of Germany on the ground that the hypothesis was unproven. Those who vituperated Bryan, and ridiculed the Kentucky Legislature, for taking substantially the same stand, might well take notice.

[2] See Dorlodot, *Darwinism and Catholic Thought* (Benziger Bros., New York, 1923).

the prerogative of making infallible decisions, nor should we who are laymen in science prejudge the findings of science. Let us take the only truly scientific position, that is, let us form our judgments strictly on the evidence presented. Let us call an hypothesis an hypothesis. If the hypothesis becomes an established fact, we shall gladly recognize the fact. We will not anticipate. There is no need of hurry. Between now and the time when, if ever, the evolutionary theory shall be demonstrated, so many modifications of its meaning may take place that it will be acceptable even to the most orthodox. Meanwhile, any theory of evolution that leaves us the right to believe in God and to call our souls our own, is welcome to a hearing. But if an evolutionist, forgetting the limitations of his science, tells us that evolution abolishes God and makes man not an immortal soul, but a chemical compound, or a mere animal, we shall repudiate him. If he tells us that our body is dust, we shall say, "We have that in our Bible." If he tells us that through the body we have kinship with the beasts, we shall say, "We know that too." But if he tells us that there is no strictly human soul animating his flesh, or if he declare that no First Cause is necessary to explain the origin of either body or soul, we shall tell him that by supposing an effect without an adequate Cause, he undermines the primary law of science, and incidentally he stultifies himself. For reason and religion and science all combine to demonstrate that, though man is kin to the animals, "A man's a man for a' that"; and that whether this dust of the body came to us directly from mother

[123]

earth, or indirectly through the beasts, there is a "spark that animates the dust." The whole mystery of man is that he is at once a brother to the animals and a child of God.

MARK TWAIN

I

If the American people were invited, in a vast plebiscite, to name their favorite author (living or dead), it is quite probable that their choice would be Mark Twain. In these days of enormous editions of "best sellers," there are, doubtless, some writers whose output—and whose income—exceed those of Mark Twain. Yet, even as far back as the late 60's and early 70's of the nineteenth century, when the machinery of advertising was still primitive, the publishers of "Innocents Abroad" sold 300,000 copies. On the title page of the first edition is the naïve announcement, "This book is not for sale in the stores. Residents of any state desiring a copy, should address the publishers and an agent will call upon them." An author who could sell several hundred thousand copies of a work under such a handicap, forty years ago, is no mean rival to our contemporary Harold Bell Wrights, Zane Greys and Irvin Cobbs. Even to-day, it is reported that Mark Twain's publishers sell over a million dollars worth of his works annually.

Judged not only by the clumsy criterion of sales and profits, but by the opinions of the critics, Mark Twain remains the leading American author. "You are the Lincoln of our literature," Mr. Howells told him; "Your foundations are struck so deep that you will catch the sunshine of the immortal years, and bask in the same light as Cervantes and Shakespeare." Rudyard

Kipling spoke of him as, "The great and Godlike Clemens," and informed the American people (with more force than elegance), "He is the biggest man you have on your side of the water, by a damn sight, and don't you forget it. Cervantes was a relation of his." Bernard Shaw declares that America has produced only two geniuses, Edgar Allan Poe and Mark Twain. Brander Matthews, following Kipling and Howells, compares Clemens with Cervantes. William Lyon Phelps maintains that Mark Twain is "one of the supreme novelists of the world." John Macy calls him "an original and powerful thinker," and H. L. Mencken gives judgment that he was "without question a great artist."

Not only as an author, but as a man and a fellow citizen, Mark Twain was almost idolatrously regarded by his contemporaries. While he was still living, one of his autographed letters was sold at auction for a higher price than those of Theodore Roosevelt, U. S. Grant, and Abraham Lincoln. On his travels abroad, as well as at home, he was considered to be the greatest of Americans. He called himself, jocosely, "Ambassador at Large of the United States." The title might well have been used in all seriousness. Again and again he was offered high diplomatic position. He always refused, but traveling without portfolio, he received such adulation as is given not to diplomats but to kings. He traveled in luxurious private cars; his baggage was at all borders exempted from inspection; and wherever he took up his residence, his apartments took on the appearance of a regal court.

Yet Mark Twain, favorite of peoples and kings

and critics, was—by a horrible paradox—an inveterate pessimist, a hater of the human race. "No man," says Gamaliel Bradford, "ever had more friends, or loved more, and no man ever abused the human heart more, or railed more at the hollowness of human affection." Clemens said of himself, "I am like Lord Byron. He despised the race because he despised himself. I feel as he did and for the same reason." A favorite expression of Mark Twain's was "the damned human race." With almost equal frequency, in his conversation, and even in his later writings, he used the expression "this mangy human race." More bitter than Dean Swift, more pessimistic than Schopenhauer, more deistic than Voltaire, more crudely and maliciously irreverent than Bob Ingersoll, he was, and is, nevertheless, the favorite and best-loved author among a cheerful, and essentially religious-minded people. Here is an anomaly that is, perhaps, beyond explanation. Yet it is less difficult to account for Mark Twain's popularity, than to solve the deep psychological riddle of his abnormally divided personality. Mr. Van Wyck Brooks (from whose volume I have been quoting rather liberally), has made a brave effort to solve that problem, by the application of the principles of a Freudian psychology. [1] Perhaps I may be permitted to attempt the less ambitious task of discovering how it came to pass that the American people, who generally give short shrift to cynics and infidels, have fallen heels-over-head in love with one who was perhaps the greatest cynic and infidel that America has produced.

[1] *The Ordeal of Mark Twain*, by Van Wyck Brooks. E. P. Dutton, 1920.

II

Mark Twain accuses himself of deliberate and prolonged concealment of his true opinions on life and man and religion. For many years, during which he gave to the publishers and to the people, many a volume of rollicking humor, he was at work secretly upon a book which he called his "bible." It occupied his spare time from 1880 until 1905. He considered it his lifework, and he meant it to be devastating. When it was ready for the press, he held it back. "Am I honest?" he wrote to one of his friends, "I tell you I am not. For seven years I have suppressed a book which my conscience tells me I ought to publish." Finally he had two hundred and fifty copies printed for distribution amongst his intimates. Later he gave it to the general public, but at first anonymously. No one suspected its authorship and it was "not over favorably received." Finally, becoming bolder, he admitted the authorship of "What is Man," and finding that his faithful readers were not too grievously shocked, he brought out a series of similarly pessimistic works.

He was constantly preparing his autobiography and according to his own promise—or threat—it was to be "as caustic, as fiendish, as devilish as can be. It will make people's hair curl." He insisted that it should not be published until a hundred years after his death, and declared that any one who violated his will in the matter deserved to be "buried alive." [1]

[1] In spite of these threats and imprecations, a few chapters of the autobiography appeared in the *North American Review*, in 1906–1907. The entire work is now published, Harpers, 1924.

This is strange language from the man who has made millions chuckle and roar with laughter. Obviously, we need a revaluation of the meaning and the importance of Mark Twain's work. The task will be an ungracious one, for the public is inclined to hate any one who criticizes its favorites. If the question be asked, "Why not let Mark Twain rest in peace— why bring to life the unedifying side of his character? Why not let the world remember him as the creator of the immortal Huckleberry Finn and Tom Sawyer?" the answer must be that neither Mark Twain nor his immediate family, nor his biographer, nor his publishers, nor his discriminating readers permit themselves the illusion that Mark Twain was primarily or principally a humorist, or a mere writer of boys' stories. He is a philosopher, wrestling constantly and desperately with the most prodigious of all philosophical mysteries, the mystery of evil. Even when he wrote stories ostensibly for children, he was preoccupied with philosophy. Paradoxically, his stories of boys are not written for boys, but for grown-ups. He says: "I wrote Tom Sawyer and Huck Finn for adults exclusively, and it always distresses me when I find that boys and girls have been allowed access to them." [1]

The sentiment, expressed in the letter, seems inconsistent with the fact that Mark Twain read *Huckleberry Finn* to his own children. The following extract from a juvenile biography of Susy Clemens, is significant: "Ever since papa and mama were married,

[1] Letter to Asa Don Dickinson, one of the librarians of the Brooklyn Public Library. Paine, *Biography*, III, 1280–1281. *Autobiography*, II, 335.

papa has written his books and then taken them to mama in manuscript, and she has expergated (Susy's spelling is preserved) them. Papa read *Huckleberry Finn* to us in manuscript (probably meaning proof), just before it came out, and then he would leave parts of it with Mama to expergate, while he went off to the study to work, and sometimes Clara and I would be sitting with mama while she was looking the manuscript over, and I remember so well, with what pangs of regret we used to see her turn down the leaves of the pages, which meant that some delightfully terrible part must be scratched out. And I remember one part particularly which was perfectly fascinating it was so terrible, that Clara and I used to delight in and oh, with what despair we saw Mama turn down the leaf on which it was written, we thought the book would almost be ruined without it. But we gradually came to think as mama did." [1] No doubt, in deprecating the influence of *Tom Sawyer* and *Huckleberry Finn* upon youthful minds, the author has reference principally to coarseness, vulgarity of the humor, and the irreverential spirit of the boys. Perhaps he would have agreed that children also should be protected from the gruesomeness continually recurring in *Life on the Mississippi*.

Gamaliel Bradford, who specializes in American biography, says "It took years to shake off the withering blight which Mark Twain's satire cast for me over the whole art of Europe.—Again, in going back to him to write his portrait, I find the same portentous

[1] Albert Bigelow Paine, *Mark Twain; a Biography*. New York. Harper and Brothers, 1912. Vol. II, pp. 774, 775.

shadowing darkness stealing over me.—I lived for ten years with the soul of Robert E. Lee, and it really made a better man of me. Six months of Mark Twain made me a worse.—I am fifty-six years old. What can he not do to boys and girls of sixteen? My final total impression of Mark Twain is desolating." One may perhaps reply that boys and girls of sixteen read a book for the story and the fun, without seeing any "philosophy," just as childish minds of twice or thrice that age read novels without in the least understanding the novelist's message. But not all boys and girls of sixteen, or of thirty, or forty, are intellectual sieves. A fair percentage of readers are advanced beyond the semi-imbecile stage. They consciously realize what they read. And perhaps another large percentage absorbs unconsciously some of the philosophy that lies lurking under the surface of the most apparently frivolous and meaningless stories of a thinker like Mark Twain.

III

If one, after youth has passed, re-reads the earliest of Mark Twain's volumes, he will find their humor amazingly crude. As Henry James says, they make their appeal to "rudimentary minds." If Henry James be considered too sophisticated to give a judgment, perhaps Mark Twain himself may be appealed to. The story that first made him famous, "The Jumping Frog of Calaveras County," he called a "villainous back-woods sketch," and he was amazed,—not to say dis-gusted—that the comparatively cultured Eastern public received it so enthusiastically. In truth, its popularity is surprising. Even James Russell Lowell called it "the finest piece of humorous writing yet produced in America." If that judgment be true, it is a pitiful indictment of American humor before 1865. Mr. Paine says "the humor of the 'Jumping Frog' is fundamental," and he feels it necessary to explain, "We were a smaller and simpler people in those days."

Mark Twain's reputation was, therefore, first achieved amongst a people who were, in the mass, unsophisticated. His "villainous backwoods sketches" appealed to a people who were only one or two generations, if at all, removed from the backwoods. Their mentality was primitive. It is safe to say that no American humorist could to-day build up a reputation on such coarse fun as that of *Innocents Abroad*. Even the cheapest vaudeville performer could hardly "get away" with such witticisms as Mark Twain makes, for example, upon Canon Fulbert, the guardian of Eloise. "Her uncle was a canon of the Cathedral. I don't know what a canon is, but that is what he was. He must have been a mountain howitzer, because they had no artillery in those days. She spent her youth in Argenteuil. I never heard of that place, but there must have been such a place. She returned to her uncle, the old gun, or the old son of a gun. His name was Fulbert. His first name is not given, let us call him George W. Fulbert." Then the great American humorist proceeds to joke about what he heard of an unnameable mutilation of Abelard. *Innocents Abroad* is in much the same vein throughout.

In St. Peter's Cathedral, Mark Twain writes of "The thing they call the baldachino, a great bronze pyramidal framework like that which upholds a mosquito-bar. It only looked like a considerably magnified bedstead, nothing more." A man who can look upon the Baldachino over the main altar of St. Peter's and think of nothing but a bedstead, is as funny as a man at the brink of the Grand Canyon, to whom it appears merely as an excavation for a cellar. The word "Baldachino" seems novel to him. So does the word "Renaissance." "Who is this Renaissance?", he asks, "and where did he come from?" When the guide points out a statue of Moses, he asks, "Moses who?" Even to-day, it must be confessed there are American travelers in Europe who think such remarks funny, but they are chiefly sophomores, or get-rich-quick-Wallingfords, or bootleggers.

Painfully it must be recorded that Mark Twain (writing in 1868) was not above condescending to the religious prejudices of the anti-Catholic section of the American public. He records the "noble conduct" of the Dominican friars during an epidemic of cholera in Naples, and he says, sweetly enough, "They must love their religion very much, to suffer so much for it." He reports that a couple of friars, on his boat to the Azores, even though for poverty's sake they traveled in the steerage, played the piano, sang grand opera, and were the "life of the ship," but then, apparently, for fear his readers at home might blame him for admitting that friars can be human, and cultured, and even heroic, he immediately calls them "barefooted rascals," and "bloody-minded sons of the Inquisition." Constantly he speaks of "Jesuit humbuggery," not because he knew of any "humbuggery" done by Jesuits, but because his public was largely of the kind that liked to hear harsh words of Jesuits.

Other evidence that Mark Twain's humor was frequently, if not habitually, coarse and vulgar, is written all over his earlier works, and is not absent even from those that came last from his pen. In *Pudd'n-head Wilson* the most attractive personality is meant to be that of Judge Driscoll. Though living in Missouri, he is an F. F. V., proud of his Virginian ancestry. In hospitality and in formal and stately manners, he kept up the old Virginia traditions. He is "fine and just and generous." "To be a gentleman, a gentleman without stain or blemish was his religion, and to it he was always faithful." "He was respected, esteemed, and beloved by all the country."

So he is presented to us by his creator, Mark Twain, but when this F. F. V., with whom gentlemanliness is a religion, goes out to make a speech in a political campaign, he speaks of the two Italian counts as "adventurous mountebanks, side-show riff-raff, dime museum freaks, back-alley barbers, peanut peddlers masquerading as gentlemen, organ grinders bereft of their brother monkey."

I have said that much of Mark Twain's early humor would not pass muster even in the cheaper vaudeville houses of to-day. I should not be surprised to learn that such humor as this would be ruled off the boards even in those rendezvous of degenerates that are called "burlesque " houses in America to-day. I rather fancy that the critics who compare Clemens with Cervantes have confounded Cervantes with Rabelais.

IV

Probably no other American author ever wrote so contemptuously as Mark Twain about the human race. His "bible," *What is Man,* is in the form of a dialogue between an old man and a young man. The old man is himself, the young man is a mere puppet, an interlocutor.

The author affirms and reaffirms (rather tiresomely to tell the truth), that man is only a machine. He says "Man is a machine, an impersonal engine. He is moved, directed, commanded, by exterior influences. He originates nothing,—not even a thought. His brain has no command over itself. Its owner has no command over it. There is no more personal merit in being brave than in being a coward. The only impulse that ever moves a person to do a thing is to content his own spirit, and win its approval. He may think he is doing it for the other person's sake, but it is not so. From his cradle to his grave a man never does a single thing which has any first and foremost object but one—to secure peace of mind, spiritual comfort for himself . . ."

Even mother-love is selfish. A mother loves her child, he explains, not for the child's sake, but primarily for her own sake. "She will go naked to clothe her child, she will starve that it may have food, suffer torture to save it from pain, die that it may live. She takes a living pleasure in making these sacrifices. She does it for that reward, that self-approval, that contentment, that peace, that comfort. She would do it for your child if she could get the same pay." . . ."Duty for duty's sake does not exist." "Love, hate, charity, compassion, avarice, benevolence, are all forms of self-contentment, self-gratification. We have smuggled a word into the dictionary which ought not to be there at all,—self-sacrifice. The sole impulse which dictates and compels a man's every act, is the imperious necessity of securing his own approval, in every emergency and at all costs. Self-approval is our breath, our heart, our blood. It is our only spur, our whip, our goad, our only impelling power. We have no other."

When the interlocutor in the book objects, "This is an *infamous* doctrine," he replies, "It is not a doctrine, it is a fact."

When the young man insists, "It is a *desolating* doctrine," "it makes of man a mere coffee mill," the old man answers, "It is correctly stated."

His chief bugbear is what he calls contemptuously, the "moral sense" of man. He pours ridicule upon the moral sense. "No one of the animals," he says, "is tainted with the disease called the 'moral sense.'" "Man," he says repeatedly, "is the meanest of animals." "If you pick up a starving dog and make him prosperous, he will not bite you. This is the principal difference between a dog and a man." If this curiously perverted and exaggerated sentence stood alone, we would say it was written as a joke. But Mark Twain is desperately in earnest in his indictment of all mankind. Here, for example, is his idea of the history of the human race.

"A myriad of men are born, they labor and sweat and struggle for bread. They squabble and scold and fight. They scramble for little mean advantages over one another. Age creeps upon them. Infirmities follow. Shames and humiliations bring down their prides and their vanities. Those they love are taken from them, and the joy of life is turned to aching grief. The burden of pain, care, misery, grows heavier year by year. At length, ambition is dead. Longing for release is in its place. It comes at last, the only unpoisoned gift earth ever had for them. They vanish from a world where they were of no consequence, where they have achieved nothing, where they were a mistake and a failure, and a foolishness, where they have left no sign that they ever existed, a world which will lament them a day, and forget them forever."

For sheer eloquence, for simple beauty of diction, that passage is obviously a classic. This is a far advance from the occasionally crude English of "Innocents Abroad." It is in the best style of Mark Twain. But, as the ingenuous youth says, "It is a desolating doctrine!" And will any admirers of Mark Twain say that this eloquent passage is an adequate picture of all human life? Is there no unselfish love? Was not Mark Twain himself loved most purely and unselfishly by his wife and children? Is death really the "only unpoisoned gift?"

Nor is the passage an isolated example of his occasional thought, a fragment dashed off in a moment of petulance or despondency. It is his habitual conviction.

"What is the difference between man and me?" says Satan, who is also God, in *The Mysterious Stranger.*—"He picked up a woodlouse that was creeping along a piece of bark, 'What is the difference between Cæsar and this?' 'Man is made of dirt. I saw him made. Man is a museum of diseases, a home of impurities. He comes to-day and is gone to-morrow. He begins as dirt, and departs as a stench.'—'Your paltry race, always lying, always claiming virtues which it hasn't got, always denying them to the higher animals, which alone possess them. No brute ever does a cruel thing,—that is the monopoly of those who have the moral sense.'" The "moral sense," which he sometimes calls the "mongrel moral sense," is Mark Twain's *bête noire.* Innumerable times he recurs to the attack upon it.

His doctrine, however, is not altogether clear. At times he seems to concede the moral sense. Again he derides the idea, insisting that man is a machine. For example, "There is no such thing as morality. It is not immoral for the tiger to eat the wolf, or the wolf the cat, or the cat the bird, and so on down.—It is not immoral for one nation to seize another nation, by force of arms, or for one man to seize another man's property or life, if he is strong enough and wants to take it. It is not immoral to create the human species, with or without ceremony. Nature intended these things." [1]

[1] Paine, *Biography,* Vol. III, p. 1335.

He denies also that man has a mind. "I will examine," he says, "what man calls his mind and give you the details of that chaos." Men "have foolish little feelings, and foolish little vanities, and impertinences and ambitions. They have no sense,—only the moral sense."

Mark Twain is curiously obsessed with the idea of microbes. "In a healthy man's lower intestines, 28 million microbes are born and die every day. In the rest of his body 122 millions, that is 150 millions in all. In ten days 1500 millions. To what end are these microbes introduced into the human race? That they may eat. Now then, according to man's own reasoning, what is man for? To furnish food for microbes." [1]

"To me," (says God) "there is no difference between man and a microbe. Man looks down upon a speck called a microbe, from an altitude of a thousand miles, I look down upon the speck called a man and a microbe, from an altitude of a million leagues, so to speak, and to me they are of a size. To me they both are inconsequential."

An equally narrow and contemptuous view of the sum of human life is quoted by Van Wyck Brooks. [2] "I have been reading the morning paper. I do it every morning, well knowing that I shall find in it the usual depravities, basenesses, and hypocrisies, and cruelties that make up civilization, and cause me to put in the rest of the day pleading for the damnation of the human race." And he had a "plan," to exter-

[1] Paine, *Biography*, Vol. III, pp. 1159–1160.
[2] Op. cit., p. 6.

minate the human race by withdrawing the oxygen from the air for ten minutes.

There may be those who are so inalterably devoted to Mark Twain that they will declare these things to be mere pleasantries. But if these mad statements be jokes, they are in a different mode from those of the *Jumping Frog*, or *Huckleberry Finn*. But no one who really reads Mark Twain thoroughly would imagine that in these diatribes he is even half jesting. He is terribly in earnest.

V

Mark Twain was not an atheist, but a Deist. In his Credo, written in the early 80's, he says, "I believe in God the Almighty," but he adds, immediately, "I do not believe He ever sent a message to man by anybody." And again he says, "No one who thinks can imagine the universe made by chance. There is, of course, a great master mind, but"—he adds—"It cares nothing for our happiness or unhappiness." [1] Obviously, this is Aristotelian paganism—Deism. Aristotle was wont to say that God in heaven could no more concern Himself with the affairs of man than a king enthroned in state could be worried about the fowl in the royal barnyard. Voltaire's idea of God's aloofness was the same. Twain probably knew nothing of Aristotle, any more than of "Renaissance." He must have got his Deism from Voltaire.

But he was less reverent than Voltaire. Thinking that God cared nothing about man, he seems to have

[1] Paine, *Biography*, III, 1353.

considered himself free to say any blasphemous thing he pleased. He told his biographers that "Mother Eddy deserves a place in the Trinity, as much as any member of it." [1] He became bolder and more violent in his denunciations of the Deity, and ended by identifying God and the devil.

The thesis of *The Mysterious Stranger* (a book written for children, and usually published with gorgeous illustrations, as suitable for a Christmas gift) is that God has no morality. The acts of God and the acts of Satan are the same. The hero of the book is called "Satan." He is a nephew of the Lucifer who fell like lightning from heaven. He is a youth of charming manners and most engaging personality. He makes himself a great favorite with the boys, and exercises his supernatural power for their amusement and their comfort. Indeed he scatters blessings throughout the whole community. But with diabolical ruthlessness, or rather with utter indifference, he inflicts calamities upon the innocent. He creates a city of little people, humans in fact, and then blots them out.

The boy who narrates the story says, "The people came flying out, shrieking, but Satan brushed them back, paying no attention to our begging and crying and imploring; and in the midst of the howling of the wind and volleying of the thunder the magazine blew up, the earthquake rent the ground wide, and the castle's wreck and ruin tumbled into the chasm, which swallowed it from the sight and closed upon it, with all that innocent life, but one of the five hundred poor

[1] Paine, *Biography*, III, 1271.

creatures escaping. Our hearts were broken, we could not keep from crying.

'Don't cry,' Satan said, 'they were of no value.'

'But they are gone to hell.'

'Oh, it is no matter; we can make plenty more.'"

He miraculously transports the boys hither and thither, even to China and the ends of the earth, but wherever they go and whatever pleasures he creates for them, he never ceases to preach to them that God has no pity, no mercy, no moral sense.

The volume contains only one hundred and fifty pages. Perhaps no one writing in English has ever crowded so much pessimism, and atheistic argument into a similar space. He concludes with a powerful but horrible paragraph:

"Strange that you should not have suspected that your universe and its contents were only dreams, visions, fiction! Strange, because they are so frankly and hysterically insane—like all dreams; a God who could make good children as easily as bad, yet preferred to make bad ones; who could have made every one of them happy, yet never made a single happy one; who made them prize their bitter life, yet stingily cut it short; who gave his angels eternal happiness unearned, yet required his other children to earn it; who gave his angels painless lives, yet cursed his other children with biting miseries and maladies of mind and body; who mouths justice and invented hell—mouths mercy and invented hell—mouths Golden Rules and forgiveness multiplied by seventy times seven, and invented hell; who mouths morals to other people and has none himself; who frowns upon crimes, yet commits them all; who created man without invitation, then tries to shuffle the responsibility for man's acts upon man, instead of honorably placing it where it belongs, upon himself; and finally, with altogether divine obtuseness, invites this poor, abused slave to worship him!'"

It is hard to recognize in this strangely perverse misinterpretation of Christian theology the words of the humorist, the genial popular favorite, the traditionally sweet-tempered, kindly Mark Twain. It is a fact, however, that though he made his name and his fortune as a humorist, he considered himself a philosopher. He was a disillusioned misanthrope, full of contempt for human nature, and of blasphemous criticism of God. His permanent system of thought seems to have been a "soulless and blasting development of crude evolutionary materialism." [1]

It is well known that he seemed to cherish a particular hatred of "Christian Science," yet his over-vigorous protestations against the ideas of Mrs. Eddy seem to indicate that he too was tempted to believe in the unreality of the universe.

"'Life itself is only a vision, a dream.' It was electrical. By God, I had had that very thought a thousand times in my musings. 'Nothing exists; all is a dream. God—man—the world—the sun, the moon, the wilderness of stars—a dream, all a dream; they have no existence. Nothing exists save empty space—and you.'

'I.'

[1] Gamaliel Bradford.

'And you are not you; you have no body—no blood, no bones, you are but a thought. I myself have no existence; I am but a dream; your dream, creature of your imagination. In a moment you will have realized this, then you will banish me from your visions and I shall dissolve into the nothingness out of which you made me.'

'Strange, that you should not have suspected years ago—centuries, ages, eons ago; for you have existed, companionless, through all the eternities. Strange, indeed, that you should not have suspected that your universe and its contents were only dreams, visions, fiction. Strange, because they are so frankly and hysterically insane—like all dreams.'" [1]

One of the articles of his early creed runs thus: "I do not see why I should be either punished or rewarded hereafter for the deeds I do now." Perhaps the unhappy philosopher felt that he was suffering enough in this life. In spite of all the honor heaped upon him, and all the adulation given him, he was wretched. "I ought to have died years ago," he said; "If I live two years more I will kill myself." He was the deepest pessimist in all America.

Mr. Howells, who after all understood him very little, thought Twain's pessimism a "pose." Mr. Paine says, rather vaguely, that he was a pessimist "by premeditation." No one who reads him thoroughly can fail to come to either one of two conclusions. Either his skepticism, his pessimism, his cynicism and his blasphemy were all pretense; or he was habitually at

[1] *The Mysterious Stranger.*

odds with the universe. The second supposition may be difficult, but the first is impossible.

If ever a man sowed what he reaped, it was Mark Twain. In youth he habitually derided religion and all those things which men normally hold sacred. In middle age, and old age he was plunged into the depths of despondency, violently disdainful of himself, the human race, and God.

ANATOLE FRANCE

I

Almost a quarter of a century ago, Edmund Gosse expressed the opinion that Anatole France was "the most interesting intelligence working in the field of letters." Similarly sweeping eulogies of the famous French ironist, have appeared in abundance ever since. "It is a rare thing in any age," says the New York *Nation* "for a man to be accepted as the world's greatest living man of letters." Yet who was there to dispute that distinction with Anatole France? Shaw or Hardy? Gorky or Brandes or Hauptmann? Anatole France stood alone." [1] In his own country, he was, we are led to believe, accepted as the peer of Villon, Rabelais, Montaigne, Voltaire, Rousseau and Renan.

When he died (October 12, 1924), one might have read hundreds of literary magazines and found nothing but expressions of superlative praise of the light that had just been extinguished. Indeed, we are forbidden to say that the light was extinguished. The English publishers of Anatole France's works [2] quote Edward Garnett, who says, confidently, "These thirty-seven volumes will be radiating light in our foggy atmosphere, when the last scrap of iron in our fleet of dreadnaughts has long rusted away." Likewise, an American newspaper editor prophesies, "Anatole France

---

[1] *The Nation*, N. Y., Oct. 22, 1924.
[2] Dodd, Mead & Co.

leaves the world a narrow shelf of novels that will die only when men are no longer interested in love and life and laughter." A humble scribe on the same journal, not to be outdone by his superior, becomes dithyrambic: "The world has lost one of its most luminous spirits. No mere words can portray the greatness of that artist. To have walked with him through the avenues of his immortal writings, brings the joy of having known the splendor of so radiant an existence." [1]

But Anatole France is more than a light of literature. His name is a rallying point of political and social liberalism. This is a curious fact, because for the greater part of his life, he lived aloof from politics, and he was temperamentally indisposed for public life. Normally, he was only a serene observer of the world-scene. He had no confidence that humanity could be improved. He thought it absurd to talk of "progress." Yet, at the time of the Dreyfus case, he burst forth from his cherished seclusion, joined hands with Emile Zola (whom he had previously held in abhorrence), and became as valiant a fighter for "justice" as the author of *J'accuse*. From that time forth, Anatole France allied himself with the forces of protest in all countries. He became an avowed Communist, and frequently sacrificed his leisure and comfort, to take upon himself the uncongenial task of haranguing the proletariat. He, the intellectual aristocrat, of refined taste and fastidious habits appeared on the platform, and even on the street corner, in company with uncouth and rabid revolutionists.

[1] *N. Y. World*, Oct. 13; *N. Y. Evening World*, October 20, 1924.

He became addicted, in turn, to Socialism, Communism, extreme Bolshevism, and Nihilism. Rather inconsistently, he protested great patriotism during the World-War. Though he was seventy years old, he asked to be given a gun and to be sent to the trenches. Remaining (of course) at home, he edited a patriotic newspaper, and even wrote an ecstatically enthusiastic book *Sur La Voie Glorieuse* ("The Path of Glory"), which has been called "one of the strangest outbursts of patriotism in literature." After the war, he became a Communist and Pacifist again. He opposed the continued occupation of the Ruhr, and urged his countrymen to be "good Europeans," rather than "good Frenchmen." Apparently, the French people were ready to forgive him any sin he might commit against Patriotism, the prime national virtue. Presumably, they were agreed, good naturedly to consider his vacillations from Patriotism to Pacifism, and from Nationalism to Nihilism, as mere idiosyncrasies.

At his funeral, amongst the tributes placed upon his coffin, was a wreath from the "Reds" of Moscow. It is doubtful, however, if Anatole France ever really enjoyed spiritual commerce with his uncouth Bolshevistic brethren. He was a Petronius rather than a Trotsky. He was a hedonist, by profession, and in practice as much an "exquisite" as Oscar Wilde. He was wealthy and loved the comforts that wealth affords. He lived in a mansion. He made no pretense of poverty. He practiced no economy. On the contrary, he was rather given to ostentation. Indeed, if his Bolshevist admirers had known the essentially aristocratic temperament of Anatole France, they might, perhaps, have sent a bomb for the Villa Saïd rather than a wreath for his tomb. Still, here in America, we have a similar anomaly. From time to time we hear of a "millionaire-Socialist," who somehow keeps in the good graces of the "wage slaves," as they persist in calling themselves. If a millionaire-Socialist, why not an aristocrat-Bolshevist?

I have called France an "exquisite." In his own home, he affected habitually a long robe, similar to a priest's *soutane*, except for its bright colors, and the richness and softness of the material. Upon his head he wore, ordinarily, a cap of vermilion velvet, "a flamboyant bonnet like those of the Florentines of the Quattrocento of Ghirlandajo." Occasionally, however, in place of the scarlet toque, he would sport a white hat beautifully embroidered, or painted, with roses. His library resembled a chapel. The windows were of stained glass. Upon shelves and tables were numerous statues of the saints, surrounding a shrine of the Blessed Virgin Mary and the Divine Child. Upon the mantels were ciboria, chalices, monstrances, patens, censers, and other instruments of worship. Indeed, to use the phrase of M. Gsell,[1] Anatole France was *"un collectioneur enragé"* of religious objects.

The house contained, it is true, other *objets d'art* quite incongruous with the paraphernalia of the sanctuary. Like some of our American impressarios, who, with serene disinterestedness, produce "Aphrodite"

[1] *Propos d'Anatole France*, p. 150.

in one season, and "The Miracle" in another, Anatole France was just as ready to surround himself with reminders of the trade of an Egyptian courtesan, as with statues of the saints, and the sacred vessels of the altar. It was a matter of moods and seasons. While writing *Thaïs*, he courted inspiration by means of exquisite sculptures, Greek heads, torsos, and nude statuettes; while producing *Lys Rouge*, he created the appropriate atmosphere with Italian faïences; for *Jeanne d'Arc* he had tapestries of the Fifteenth Century, and for *Les Dieux Ont Soif*, furniture and engravings of the period of Louis XVI and the Revolution. His *attrait*—one might almost say obsession—for ecclesiastical ornamentation ill befits his unbelief, but not more so than his love of luxury negates his Bolshevism.

I shall leave the radicals to wrestle with the mystery of Anatole France, luxurious Socialist, and voluptuous Communist. To account for the other anomaly, that of a confirmed skeptic's *penchant* for ecclesiastical dress and ornament, as well as for theology and hagiology, I may perhaps venture a theory. He was not merely a skeptic; he was a Latin skeptic. And your Latin skeptic seldom, if ever, succeeds in liberating himself from the influence of religion. He hates religion, but cannot leave religion alone. He denies God, but he blasphemes God. He detests and ridicules the Church, but the stamp of the Church is on his soul. He is fascinated, beguiled, charmed, hypnotized, by what he hates.

When Anatole France was a boy, he resolved (like

all boys of the Latin races) to be a saint. Sometimes he would be St. Aloysius, the altar-boy's model; at another time, St. Jerome, the cave-dweller, or Saint Anthony, the hermit. He fasted, wore a hair shirt, and even attempted to live on the top of a pillar, like St. Simeon Stylites. He read of the Fathers of the Desert, and promptly became a recluse, making a Thebaid of a labyrinth in the *Jardin des Plantes*. After such a boyhood (shall we say, as might be expected), he became an unbeliever, an inveterate lampooner of religion, a caricaturist of saints, of archangels and of God. This impious sequel to an over-pious boyhood is a curious phenomenon, but it is not unusual in Latin countries. Voltaire, Diderot, Renan, and a thousand lesser infidels, as well as Anatole France, had not only a religious but a pious boyhood.

With Anatole France, antipathy to religion is a mania. Those who call him a gentle skeptic, merely because he uses the delicate instrument of irony, rather than the sledge-hammer of argument, in his attack upon faith, mistake the man. His manner is gentle, but his purpose is militant. He has the relentless energy of a zealot, and the unflagging enthusiasm of a crusader against religion. His skepticism, however, is not entirely instinctive. It is cultivated, and it needs constant encouragement. He feels it necessary to justify his unbelief. "They call me skeptic," he says. "For them it is the worst injury; for me it is the most beautiful praise. All the masters of French thought have been skeptics; Rabelais, Montaigne, Molière, Voltaire, Renan; all the great minds of the race, all those whom

I venerate with awe, and of whom I am only the humble pupil." [1]

Evidently, his list of masters of French thought is "hand-picked." No French critic will agree with him that Pascal, Bossuet, Racine, Lamartine, Chateaubriand, and a hundred other masters, may be so summarily disposed of. The proposition "all the great minds of the race were skeptics" needs no refutation. The truth is that Anatole France is not sure of his skepticism. He really doubts his own doubt. He protests too much. And he is inconsistent. He constantly sets forth the idea that saints are imbeciles. Yet he calls his greatest hero "Saint Renan." He considers priests to be charlatans or simpletons; yet he boasts "Renan was always the priest." He is not even sure of his hedonistic philosophy, or quite content with voluptuous living; he claims that Renan was an ascetic and counts it to his honor. He never really succeeds in ridding himself of his early Christian convictions. The instinct for Catholicism remains in him like the "indelible character" of a sacrament, under all the rubbish and filth of irreligion and indecency.

No critic of Anatole France can afford to neglect this psychological fact: a Latin unbeliever is always in danger of backsliding into faith. He can be loyal to his unbelief only by constantly encouraging himself to doubt. He must periodically strengthen his skepticism by mad statements, such as "All leaders of French thought were skeptics," "All great minds were skeptics."

[1] Gsell, *Propos d'Anatole France*, p. 81.

II

Hence it is that almost all the works of Anatole France are saturated with religious interest. He is as much concerned with angels and archangels as any mediæval theologian. He discourses of the three hierarchies and the nine choirs of angels, as glibly as Suarez or Aquinas. The difference between the novelist and the theologians, is that the novelist inserts his theology into the midst of the story of a *liaison*, and, of course, he makes angels ridiculous instead of sublime.

He is fascinated also by the stories of the Fathers of the Desert, and the penitents they converted. He borrows characters and corrupts them. Whatever he touches becomes vile. His *Thaïs* is a distortion of St. Mary of Egypt; his Paphnutius (who, in the novel, saves the soul of the courtesan but loses his own), was in real life St. Paphnutius who actually lived and died, "in the odor of sanctity." Naturally, the French novelist dresses up the story to suit the libidinous curiosity of his readers. A Paphnutius confirmed in grace would make no appeal to France's constituency. But a Paphnutius fallen tickles their fancy and justifies their sins.

It is customary with those who are more concerned with popularity and profit than with truth, to "give their readers what they like." When Emile Zola, for instance, takes a character from real life (Marie Lebranchu) and narrates her cure at the pool of Lourdes, he is compelled to make her relapse and die, because he knows his skeptical friends will not bear the actual truth that she remained cured. So, it would never do for Anatole France to bring Paphnutius in from the Desert to convert a courtesan, and then send him back to the Desert undefiled. There is nothing piquant about that. Paphnutius must be ruined. So the sinner is saved, and the saint is damned. There's a story. It serves the novelist's purpose. It pleases his *clientèle*. Incidentally, it libels an actual historical saint, but that is a bagatelle. It is like writing of St. Peter, and making him guilty of the sin of Judas Iscariot, or of George Washington and fastening upon him the crime of Benedict Arnold. Would such tales as these be in bad taste? Anatole France, with all his fastidiousness, thinks not. His readers apparently agree with him. Some simple folk think it almost as bad to libel a saint as to libel a patriot, but simple folk butter no parsnips for Anatole France. He may safely be trusted to know who puts the bread into his mouth, who embroiders the roses on his white cap, and who pays for the Italian faïence.

If he had simply narrated the historical *liaison* of Alexander the Great and the original Thaïs, or that of Antony and Cleopatra, it would have given his *blasé* readers no thrill. It is no news to them that an emperor or a Roman triumvir is compact of the same clay as a *boulevardier*. But take a hermit out of his cave, send him on a mission to convert a woman, and drive the devil out of her into him, tell the story skillfully and saucily and you may wheedle another three francs out of the most jaded addict of French novels.

Anatole France did not discover the device of throwing in a dash of religion to make insipid adultery piquant. Rabelais knew it. Boccaccio rang the changes on it. Dozens of French novelists and playwrights have used a modification of it. It has long been common property amongst the Latin races,—even the crude native "movies" in Mexico and South America employ it, after vulgarizing it. The formula is simple enough: instead of taking a layman for your *roué*, take a priest or a saint, or an angel. The trick has not yet been widely popularized in America or England. Protestants, or ex-Protestants, who form the bulk of the English reading public, are not familiar with the saints and the angels, and besides, they have lingering scruples of Puritanism. Catholics, too, in English-reading countries, would be a little squeamish about interlarding the lives of the saints with "saucy" stories. But Anatole France's following has no squeamishness and no scruples. When their master takes the story of Joseph and Potiphar's wife out of its atmosphere, and does it over, *more Gallico*, they are delighted. Stories from the Bible and from the lives of the saints are his stock in trade; and he knows how to dress them up and arrange them in a way that was never intended by the biblical writers. When Anatole France has rearranged the story, it will be no longer useful as a stimulus to compunction or contrition. But it will serve the purpose of tickling the *libido* of even the *blasé* Parisian *roué*. Like a few others of his compatriots, he could even have taken a horrible thing—let us say the bloody head of John the Baptist upon a platter, and use it to emphasize the feeling of delectation produced by the twinkling toes of

Salome. What higher and nobler art can there be than that?

No one, however, but Anatole France could have contrived the ridiculous and sacrilegious plot of *La Revolte des Anges*. Maurice, while at *rendezvous* with a married woman, suddenly sees a young man standing in the room. The young man turns out to be Maurice's guardian angel. A preposterous scene follows: the angel explains that he has read "all the bibles of the world" and has lost his faith. The adulterer and adulteress try to persuade him to believe again, and to reform—but in vain. The angel, after much theological argument, drifts away into the low haunts of the great city. He becomes an *habitué* of cabarets. He constantly meets other angels, rebels like himself. One of them, speaking of a dancer, complains, "The insidious movements of this creature produced in me an unknown emotion. I grew pale. I flushed. My tongue grew dry in my mouth. I could not move." A thousand French novelists put statements like that into the mouths of men. Anatole France puts them into the mouth of an angel. Little happy thoughts of that sort help to explain why the Academy calls him "Master."

Maurice, conscience-stricken for having given bad example to his guardian angel, seeks Arcadius (the angel) incessantly, through all the resorts of low life and of vice. He inserts a notice in the "Personal" column of the newspapers: "Arcadius, return to Maurice!" At last he finds Arcadius, and asks him to be once more his heavenly guardian. Arcadius refuses. Maurice says, "Then I will be your guardian angel," and the two go out together to an oyster supper. Maurice consults a priest, to learn how he may bring the angel back to the faith. Nightly, thereafter, man and angel sup together with *filles de joie*, and argue religion. Between discussions of the next great prize-fight, or a new play, Maurice tries to persuade Arcadius of the existence of God, the necessity of religion and the beauty of Christianity.

The angel quotes Darwin and Lamarck, envies men their scientific knowledge, laments that the angels, in heaven and on earth, know so little of physics and chemistry, and predicts that when they finally learn of the atoms and of ether, when they see themselves "lost between two infinities," when they become able like men to take the temperature of the sun, weigh the earth and measure the distance between the stars, they will rebel against God, and cast Him into hell.

Finally, three hundred angels meet together in an abandoned entertainment hall, and plan an assault upon God. Some of them fear the might of God, but others harangue the crowd, explaining that God is helpless because His weapons are antiquated. The assault is made, the rebels being armed with the latest implements of modern warfare. The defenders of heaven fight with weapons of the days of Abraham. St. Michael knows no other kind of battle than hand-to-hand conflict. He marshals his chariots as Pharaoh did. He hasn't even heard of the Macedonian Phalanx. The assault is successful. God flees, and with Him the queen of heaven, resting on the arm of St. Michael. The black flag of Satan enters heaven. St. Michael lays down his flaming sword at the feet of Satan. Satan is crowned God, and all the thrones and principalities and powers swear loyalty to the new God. God, in turn, becomes Satan.

Satan being now God, becomes pitiless. He looks upon suffering and death as happy effects of His omnipotence and His sovereign goodness. The blood of victims arises before Him like an agreeable incense. He condemns knowledge and proscribes intellectual curiosity. He is pleased to surround Himself with mystery, and affects to be incomprehensible. Theology takes possession of His mind and, after reflection, He declares Himself to be one God in three persons. Looking down from His heavenly throne He sees the former God, now Satan, chained in hell, and he rejoices. Satan, on the other hand, becomes filled with pity and benevolence.

There is, of course, much more of this. Satan founds his church at Rome, and gives the keys of his kingdom to the pope. The pope speaks the Our Father, addressing it now to Satan, the new God, 'hallowed be *thy* name, *thy* kingdom come, *thy* will be done."

To any one who retains a shred of Christian feeling, this is the acme of sacrilege. Readers of Anatole France must be horribly *blasé* if they need such atrocious blasphemy to get a thrill out of their reading.

If one has arrived at such a condition of theological Nihilism that "God" means nothing; if one is satisfied to have the Name and the Person of Jesus Christ bandied about and ridiculed, such a one may perhaps enjoy the burlesques of Anatole France, without reserve and without compunction. Even that, however, is doubtful, for it would seem that any one who values good taste, and common decency in literature, must feel at least some few pangs of displeasure over the work of a novelist who constantly outrages good taste, who holds nothing sacred, who identifies good with evil, and God with the Prince of Devils. As for the un-principled writer of such mad travesties, it would seem that he has made use of theology, only to revile God; he has read the lives of saints only to ridicule them; he has mingled with Christians and has minutely recorded in his memory, or in his notebooks, the faults and foibles of his fellows, so that he may pitilessly lampoon them. Surely, he is as despicable as the guest who accepts hospitality, spies upon the members of the household, mercilessly distorts their deeds and their motives, writes his data down in a book and sells it. He may succeed enormously. He may dwell in a handsome villa ornamented like a regal chapel; he may wear a scarlet toque and a rose-embroidered robe; he may surround himself with priceless bits of art; he may affect an æsthetic interest in the furnishings of the sanctuary; he may become famous throughout the world for his skill in welding words together, but to people of refined instincts, whether they have religion or not, he is a viper.

III

L'Ile des Pingouins, is a travesty on the life of a missionary saint. Saint Mael, disciple of St. Gall, being so near-sighted as to be almost blind, baptizes a flock of penguins, thinking them to be men and women. When the news of the mistake becomes known in heaven, it causes neither joy nor sorrow, but surprise. God Himself is puzzled. He calls an assembly of Doctors of Divinity, and puts to them the question of the validity of the baptism. St. Augustine, St. Patrick, Pope St. Damasus, Tertullian, and others, get enmeshed helplessly in the discussion. St. Catherine of Alexandria, who in her life on earth, knew all the wisdom of Plato, as well as that of the gospels, and who had single-handed overcome fifty theologians, extricates the learned saints and doctors from their entanglement. The penguins are to be instructed in civilization and religion.

Having thus introduced his theme, Anatole France proceeds to poke fun at all the institutions of civilization. The penguins learn to wear clothing,—(one may imagine what cope that gives to France's penchant for immodesty); they establish laws; they make a census; they lay down rules for property holding. Simultaneously they learn theft, and lying, and murder. The greatest murderers and thieves become the greatest landowners, founders of famous houses. Saint Mael lays his hands in blessing upon the most powerful of these robbers and he becomes king. The saint prays, nevertheless, that there may be no more murder and theft. His assistant evangelist, a monk named Bullock, says, "What you call 'murder' and 'theft,' is really 'war' and 'conquest,' the foundation of all Empires, the source of all virtues and of all human greatness."

The tale might perhaps be taken as a mere satire on human society, if Anatole France had been only a littérateur, amusing himself and his readers with a *jeu d'esprit*. But when we remember that this is the man who was sufficiently in earnest to abandon his ease and speak in filthy halls and on street corners, in favor of Bolshevism and Nihilism, the humor becomes a bit dubious; and when its author says, half in jest but wholly in earnest, "The only and unique origin of property is force" (a plagiarism of Proudhon's *La Propriété c'est le vol*), it may be well to remember that the gentle jester is at heart an anarchist. It is doubtful if the delegation from Moscow, who placed the wreath on the grave of Anatole France, thought that he wrote *L'Ile des Pingouins* just for the fun of the thing.

IV

It was perhaps a logical necessity that Anatole France should write on St. Joan of Arc. The lives of the saints fascinated him, and here was a saint—the favorite saint of the French people—whose supernatural glory he could dim, by going over her history again, and explaining her personality and her career, in terms of the basest and ugliest of all philosophies, psychoanalysis.

He approached the subject with great care and long preparation. He read all accounts of the career of *La Pucelle*, and arrived at the conclusion that they were all useless as historical documents. "If we knew," he says, "only what the French chroniclers tell us concerning Joan of Arc, we should know her about as well as we know Sakya-Muni." [1] On the other side, the Burgundians were equally unreliable. "The Chroniclers of that period," he explains, "French as well as Burgundian, were hired writers." [2] Supplementing the work of the hired chroniclers, there are "sets of stories, that are more disordered than the clouds of a stormy sky." As for Joan's own statements, they are of little assistance to an historian so zealous for truth as Anatole France, for he says "her perpetual hallucinations usually made her unable to distinguish the true from the false." This particular accusation, against the maid herself, is annulled by Anatole France when, on a neighboring page of the introduction to his work he says, "We all know the value of the answers of the maid: they are heroically candid, and usually transparently clear." Here is the first of a host of inconsistencies and contradictions into which he falls. She was "*usually* unable to distinguish the true from the false," yet she was "*usually* heroically candid and transparently clear."

France protests, "I have raised no doubt concerning the sincerity of Joan. No man can suspect her of lying." So he says in the preliminary dissertation,[3] but when he gets well into the work, he accuses his heroine of what is perhaps the worst form of untruth,—deliberate religious imposture. "That ravished air was not an ecstasy: it was a sham ecstasy."[4] Apparently he ap-

---

[1] *Vie de Jeanne d'Arc*, Vol. I, p. 15, Paris, Colmann Levy.
[2] *Ibid.*, p. 4.
[3] Vol. I, p. xxxviii.
[4] Vol. I, p. 391.

proves of Dunois who "would lead us to believe that the young peasant girl was a clever imposter, and gave at the request of the nobles, an exhibition of ecstasy." It would seem that he ought to remember, at least throughout the first volume, what he says in his preface. Andrew Lang, after a careful analysis of France's biography of the maid, sums up the contradictions: "The maid is honest and dishonest, simple and a cheat; in battle a leader and not a leader; in council listened to and not listened to; an adviser never regarded. . . . and an adviser constantly consulted." It is doubtful if the French chronicler, or the Burgundian, or even the writers of the "disordered sets of stories," are more confusing than Anatole France.

It is fair to conclude with the chivalrous Scot who defended the maid against her own countryman, "These examples of M. France's inconsistencies may suffice to prove that he has really produced no living and recognisable portrait of the maid." [1]

V

Obviously, it is impracticable, in one essay, to attempt an analysis of the remainder of the "thirty-seven volumes that will be forgotten only when men are no longer interested in life and love and laughter." It must suffice, by way of concluding, to call attention to what I take to be the predominating characteristics of his work;—first his perpetual preoccupation with lubricity, and second, his skepticism, or (to use the more strictly appropriate word) cynicism. His inter-

[1] Andrew Lang: *Fortnightly Review*, London, June, 1908.

est in lasciviousness seems to have been ineradicable. It remained even into his old age. High literary art and pornography are generally supposed to be separate, but Anatole France, the supreme artist, could be, and frequently was, as coarse, I will not say as Rabelais, but as *L'Asino*, or *Le Rire*. Decency prevents the setting forth of examples in proof of that statement, but no honest reader of France will deny that it is true. All manner of impurity may be found in his novels, including the sort that indicates degeneracy.

Even the Sadist can find in these treasuries of nastiness, something to gratify his degenerate instincts. Out of hundreds of instances, perhaps we can stomach one or two. "She loved him" (Gamelin, another Robespierre) "with all her flesh, and the more terrible, cruel, atrocious, he appeared; the more she saw him covered with the blood of his victims, the more she hungered and thirsted for him." "Send me to the guillotine" (she cries), "cut off my head. And at the thought of the knife on her neck, her whole body dissolved with horror and voluptuousness." [1]

Just one more curious sentence, indicative of his peculiarly perverse way (I know not what psychopathic term to use in describing it), of looking at the simplest and sweetest things, "Tout ce que les paiens ont imaginé d'impudicités monstrueuses est depassé par la plus simple fleur des champs, et si vous saviez les fornications des lis et des roses, vous ecarteriez des autels ces calices d'impureté, ces vases de scandale!" There is a familiar maxim, "To the pure all things are pure."

[1] *Les Dieux Ont Soif.*

That maxim is not true. It suggests, however, one that is true. "To the impure all things are impure," even lilies and roses.

VI

The philosophy of Anatole France is not truly to be described as a serene and kindly skepticism. How it came to pass that his view of life has gained favor in the world of letters and learning, can be explained only by those who know intimately the tacit coalition of publishers and critics, the power of a literary tradition once started; and the tendency of radicals in all countries to patronize and eulogize one another.

Brotteaux, in *Les Dieux Ont Soif*—(of course, Brotteaux here, like M. Bergeret, Jerome Coignard and many others, is Anatole France himself)—says, "John Jacques Rousseau pretended to learn his ethics from nature. He really learned it from Calvin. Nature teaches us to devour one another, and she gives us the example of all the crimes and all the vices which the state either attempts to correct or winks at. One should love virtue, but it is well to remember that virtue is merely an expedient contrived by men to enable them to live comfortably together. What we call morality is nothing but a desperate attempt of our fellowmen to overcome the law of the universe, which is conflict, carnage, and the interaction of blind and contrary forces. Nature destroys herself, and the more I think of it, the more I am convinced that the universe is mad. The theologians and philosophers who make

God the author of Nature and the architect of the Universe, make Him appear absurd and wicked. They call Him good because they fear Him, but they are compelled to admit that He acts savagely. They bestow upon Him a wickedness rare even among men. And that is the way that they make Him adorable on earth. Our miserable race would vow no worship to just and merciful gods." [1]

One must be strangely partisan to detect serenity or sweetness in that philosophy. It is a philosophy of desperation Anatole France is like a man imprisoned, who after many loud cries for help, and much beating at granite walls and iron bars, bruised and bleeding, lapses into the quiet of despondency.

Now it may be relatively true that nature is cruel. It would, however, be only fair to add that she is also kind. She destroys but she repairs. She lets loose tornadoes and cyclones and earthquakes. But she always mends the harm she has done. She even repairs the damage done by man. She has already covered up, with wheat and fruit and flowers, the ugly gashes made in the earth at the Marne, to say nothing of her everlasting patience in a hundred times draping her mantle of green and gold over the battlefields of Sicily and Flanders. Let us be just and say that nature is not altogether wicked.

Others before Anatole France have recognized the cruelty of life. They, however, have done their best to find some trifling consolation for the race in this vale of tears. His contribution to the alleviation of human

[1] *Les Dieux Ont Soif*, p. 88.

suffering, is the bitter pill of cynicism, coated with a tolerance of sexual license.

"His criticism is incessant, dissolving and destructive," says Brander Matthews.[1] He has never let the scalpel and microscope fall from his hands. "He is a frank pagan, with a paganism, through which Christianity has filtered, leaving only an impalpable deposit. . . . He is a pessimistic anarchist." Surely, a serene and smiling skeptic is one thing, but, a pessimistic anarchist is, as Mr. Perlmutter might say, "something else again."

VII

His theory of morals may be found on every second or third page of any of his writings. It never varies much from the statement in *L'Ile des Pingouins*. "The moral law obliges men, who are animals, to live otherwise than animals, which is a contradiction to them, but also flatters and comforts them. They submit freely to restraints which appeal to their vanity, and on which they build their present security and their future happiness. Such is the principle of all morality." [2]

Sorrow for sin he considers not only absurd but immoral. He finds fault with St. Augustine, because that illustrious penitent hates his sins. "Nothing spoils a confession like repentance," says France. But "poor great Jean Jacques Rousseau acknowledged his own faults and those of other people with marvellous

[1] *The Outlook*, N. Y., Nov. 30, 1921.
[2] *L'Ile des Pingouins*, p. 50.

facility. It cost him nothing to tell the truth. However vile and ignoble it might be, he knew that he could render it touching and beautiful."

Like all modern skeptics, France has a particular hatred for the Christian religion. There is a reason, not so much philosophical as æsthetic, for his hate. "He hates Christianity," says W. L. George, "because he fears its ascetic spirit. Above all, he is an æsthete and a voluptuary. He believes that pleasure is the reason of life, and that the only duties of man are to enjoy, to procure enjoyment, to foster art. In every one of his books runs his delight in color, forms, smiling lips, sweet scents, wine, dances, flower garlands . . . his natural impulse is to lay a cake of honey and a wreath of marigolds on a little altar in the forest, round which Pan might play while the Napææ dance." [1]

The misfortune about this beautiful program of human life is that it has been tried and found wanting. The piping of Pan and Napæan dancing will not make life less miserable. To think that they will, is to trust to the one great illusion. The Egyptians and the Greeks and the Romans tried that remedy for the *tædium vitæ*, and their last state became worse than their first.

> "On that hard pagan world, despair
>   And secret loathing fell
>   When deep weariness and sated lust
>   Made human life a hell."

If Anatole France had been blessed with the vision

[1] W. L. George, in the *Anglo French Review*, quoted in the *Living Age*, Aug. 9, 1919.

of a prophet, or the wisdom of an apostle, he would have understood the profound truth of the paradox, "If you live according to the flesh you shall die. But if by the spirit you mortify the deeds of the flesh, you shall live." Those that make a business of happiness are never happy. Those that welcome suffering, obtain great peace of heart.

This is truth. But Anatole France has no confidence in truth. "There is no truth in the souls of savage beasts," he says, "there is none in ours, and the metaphysicians who have described it, are lunatics. I love truth. I believe that humanity has need of it, but surely it has a much greater need of falsehood, which flatters and consoles and gives infinite hopes. Without falsehood, humanity would perish of despair and ennui." [1]

There is the last word of the philosophy of the "genial skeptic!" We are saved not by truth but by falsehood. Rather we are *not* saved. There is no salvation. Life is misery, and there is no release from misery. All that men can do to alleviate the pain of life and of thought is to shun the truth, flatter themselves with illusions, and indulge the flesh.

In fine, the conclusion of the gospel of Anatole France is cynicism in philosophy, sexual license in ethics, and nihilism in politics. Yet his adoring friends call him not only the greatest literary artist of the age, but the "Savior of Society."

We, however, the small minority, who have refused

[1] *La Vie en Fleur, The Dial,* N. Y., December, 1921, pp. 379-98; 561-80; 675-92.

to be swept off our feet by the successive waves of eulogy that have flowed over the literary world, first when Anatole France was admitted to the Academy, again when he received the Nobel Prize, and for the third time when he died; we who have not been beguiled by the conspiracy to conceal the truth about this "most interesting mind in the field of letters," are still persuaded that his fame is superficial and perishable. "He is a destroyer. This will, of itself, place him irrevocably in the lower walks of literature. Supreme greatness in a writer is not distinguished by deadliness of destruction, but of life-giving creativeness." [1]

[1] John L. Hervey, *The Catholic World*, Oct., 1918.

I

Tertullian's famous saying, "*Anima humana naturaliter Christiana*," is only half the truth. The reverse proposition is equally true, "*Anima humana naturaliter pagana*." Human nature is simultaneously Christian and pagan. "Great Pan is dead," cried the voice carried on the winds, to the Mediterranean mariner, on the first Good Friday. But legends, like oracles, are cryptic, or double-meaning. The pagan sea captain presumably imagined that the God of nature died when the sun was darkened and the earth trembled. A Christian may interpret the preternatural message as a declaration that the pagan deities, the gods of the gentiles, were slain by the death of Christ, and that when Christ rose, He rose alone, to be Lord of the world.

But if that be the sense, Pan is *not* dead. In many lands the false gods have hardly yielded an inch. And even in the Christian world, paganism remains, and periodically becomes more vigorous. The lament of the modern pagan poet,

> "Thou hast conquered, O pale Galilean,
> And the world has grown gray with thy breath,"

is untrue in both its parts. Our Savior is not the undisputed Conqueror (more's the pity), and if the world has grown gray, it is surely not from the breath of the "pale Galilean." Milton, the Christian, proclaims exultantly what Swinburne, the pagan, confesses reluctantly:

> "Peor and Baalim . . .
> And mooned Ashtaroth . . .
> The Libyc Hammon . . .
> And sullen Moloch . . .
> The brutish gods of Nile . . .
> Isis, and Orus and the dog Anubis,
> . . . Osiris . . . "

and the whole "damned crew" of gods and goddesses fled when Christ appeared.

But when we emerge from the ecstasy of poetry to the somber reality of facts, we must admit that these triumphant proclamations of the victory of Christ over the devil-gods, are true only as desires and perhaps as prophecies.

No! Pan is not dead. Paganism still fights stubbornly and retreats very slowly. Missionaries may push back the frontiers of the kingdom of Satan a trifle, but meanwhile Satan-worship bursts forth spasmodically at home.

I do not mean to say that paganism is thrusting out Christianity. I do not even think that paganism is to a great degree demoralizing Christianity. But Christianity and paganism run side by side in our world. Let me illustrate. Those who have traveled on that most beautiful of all rivers, the St. Lawrence, will perhaps remember a striking phenomenon that occurs at the junction of the St. Lawrence and the Ottawa. The larger stream is crystal-clear, and blue as the tropical seas. The smaller stream is often tawny with silt. The two meet and run along together, but quite distinguishable from each other. Ultimately, of course, the greater river purifies and absorbs the smaller. But for some miles there is the curious spectacle of a clear blue river, and a muddy brown one, running side by side in the same bed, between the same banks. So, it seems to me, Christianity and paganism course along, side by side, in modern society. Our Christianity, generally speaking, is as pure as it was at any time since the days of the Apostles. Our paganism is almost as foul as it was in the days of the Renaissance, almost as noxious as in the times of the Cæsars.

I suppose it is scarcely necessary for me to say that, when I speak of "pagans," I do not mean savages—"heathens," in the sense of that word as we find it in missionary literature. Heathens, indeed, are pagans, but not all pagans are heathens. We do not speak of Fiji Islanders and Tierra del Fuegans, of Maoris, or aboriginal American Indians. Our modern pagans are not savages.

Again, when I say "pagans," I do not mean barbarians. I shall not speak of the kind of paganism that prevailed in Britain and Scandinavia and Germany and Scythia, before Europe was evangelized and civilized. It would be ridiculous to compare our modern pagans with the Goths, the Vandals, the Lombards, and the Huns. One may be convinced that these moderns will destroy civilization just as surely as did the barbarians, but they will not destroy it with fire and sword, with pillage and rapine and plunder. They will destroy civilization with the arts of civilization.

In a word, we are concerned with polite pagans, civilized pagans, in some cases of very nice culture, of high intelligence, and of great education. Our pagans are after the manner of Antony and Cleopatra, of Cæsar and Seneca, of Horace and Petronius, of Lucullus and Mæcenas, of Poggio and Boccaccio, rather than of Attila, or Genghis Khan, or the Sultan of Sulu, or Sitting Bull. In a word, our modern paganism is another Renaissance, a recrudescence of the paganism of the golden age of Augustus and Tiberius Cæsar; and especially of the later Roman Empire, when civilization rose so high that it toppled over; when culture became so ripe that it turned rotten; a paganism that was concomitant with the highest civilization and the basest corruption that the world has ever seen.

II

Now, there were two kinds of Greco-Roman paganism—popular and philosophical; and I think that in our days we have a recurrence of both of them.

First, there is popular paganism. It is the paganism of the languorous Orient, such as you find it in the *Rubaiyat* of Omar Khayyám. In the latter days of Rome this Oriental paganism was imported into the West. The old Romans had been simple, virile, austere; but their descendants became soft, and yielded to the luxuriousness of the East. Baal and Ashtaroth, Venus and Adonis—and Bacchus—became the popular deities. To eat, and to drink, and to play, became the occupation of the people. Horace, the aristocrat, "hated the vulgar horde," yet gave the masses an ignoble motto: "Seize pleasure while it flies; it is a gift divine"—meaning by "pleasure" such things as cannot be called by their right names in a Christian assembly. In the later Empire, there was developed an æsthetic paganism, a gay, glad, mad paganism, a *joie de vivre* paganism. It was the paganism that exulted in revels, in orgiastic excitement; the paganism that glorified and deified and idolized the human body.

There, perhaps, is the distinguishing note of paganism, ancient and modern. It concentrates its attention upon the body and bodily pleasures. It is greedy of sense enjoyments. It craves the satisfaction of the eye, with beauty, color, form; it abhors what is ugly, but it welcomes what is suggestive and even lascivious. It seeks satisfaction for the ear: dulcet sounds, languishing melodies, appealing rhythms, that titillate the nerves, gently intoxicate the blood, that set the body to swaying. It is the paganism of the nude in art, the sensuous in music, the suggestive and the daring in literature.

In our days particularly, it is manifest in the cabarets, in musical "*Revues,*" in "Follies" and "Vanities," and "Scandals" and "Passing Shows." It is the paganism of brilliant spectacles, of artistic nakedness, of tortuous and fantastic dancing—dancing that centers about and suggests and insinuates the sex relation. It is the paganism of delicate foods and delicious drinks. It is the paganism that makes a religion of eating and drinking. It is the paganism of an ever-increasing exposure of the body, by those who dress themselves as a provocation to passion rather than a protection against shame.

In ancient days this kind of paganism was symbolized in the Greco-Roman sculpture; in the Venus of Medici, if not the Venus of Milo, in the Apollo Belvedere, in Cupids and Bacchantes—faultless bodies, sometimes softly alluring, sometimes again frantically exciting.

In our days the popular type of paganism is symbolized perhaps best by what is called classical dancing, which emphasizes nudity, flouts Christian modesty, and glories in *abandon*. In a word, popular paganism is the worship of the body and the cult of all that belongs to the body.

Over against all this, now as of old, stands Christianity, with its symbol of the Cross, the mangled, bruised, bleeding body of Jesus Christ hanging transfixed. St. Paul declared it to be a stumbling-block to the Greeks. It is a scandal and a horror to our modern pagans. Show them a Crucifix, and they will cry, "Take away the hideous, horrible thing!"

When the Apostles descended upon Rome and Ephesus and Corinth, where luxury and pleasure ran riot, they were proscribed, not because they preached a new religion—there were a dozen new religions in the Empire every year; not because they preached a strange religion—Rome was excessively tolerant of all the exotic, bizarre religions that swarmed in from the Orient; no, Christianity was hated, detested, prosecuted, as a kill-joy religion. The Christians were called *ini-*

and Health," inculcates neither prayer nor worship of God.

As with "Christian Science," so with all modern New Thought "religions." They might better be called philosophies, invented or reconstructed by simple people who imagined themselves adepts in metaphysics, but who really had only a penchant for philosophical speculation, and who, in working over and attempting to popularize some doctrine of metaphysics, have only made it grotesque and incredible. Then, naturally, it passes, amongst untrained minds, for religious mystery.

A second salient feature of the philosophies that men accept in place of a discarded religion, is that they must be new, or at least have the semblance of novelty. When St. Paul came to Athens, he found the Academicians on the Areopagus engaged in what purported to be philosophical discussion, as their forbears had been in the days of Plato and Socrates. But there was a peculiar feature about the philosophy of the decadent Greeks. Having abandoned the old orthodox philosophies which had been in vogue for four hundred years, they craved some *new thing*, some philosophical novelty. The Acts of the Apostles says, "The Athenians employed themselves in nothing else, but either in telling or in hearing some new thing." And, as always in days of decadence, the stranger the doctrine, the better were they pleased.

If St. Paul had given them some novel and fantastic philosophy, he might have won them.

Let us suppose,—even though the supposition be

fantastic,—that he had addressed them in this fashion:

"Ye men of Athens, I am come to preach to you Oriental idealism. I have received it from the Mahatmas who dwell in inaccessible monasteries perched high upon the mountains between India and Tibet. Hearken to what I have to say. Hearken, ye men of Athens, to the philosophy of the East! Nothing is that is. All that is, is not. All that is not, is. Observe yon marble statue; it has no real existence, it is not there. See that solid pillar; there is no pillar. All that is, is Mind. All that is, is in the Mind. The benches whereon ye sit—they are not there. The earth beneath your feet—there is no earth beneath your feet. The men you see around about you—they exist only in your mind. They are but modifications of your ego. I seem to speak to you, and you seem to listen to me. But there is no I, or you. There is only Mind. I am but communing with my own consciousness. You are not there, I am not here. I speak, but I speak not. You hear, but you do not hear. There is no hearing. There is no speaking. There is no statue. There is no temple. There are no men. There is only Mind.

"And yet again, ye men of Athens, hearken, even though ye cannot hear. There is no pain. No sickness. There can be no sickness. No death   Death is but a delusion of mortal mind."

If he had recited this metaphysicaı nonsense slowly, solemnly, and with a mystic chant; if he had rolled his eyes and softly modulated his voice; if he had spoken his message to the accompaniment of excellent music, his hearers might have cried out, "Hail, wiser than Socrates; hail, profounder than Plato; hail, prince of philosophers!"

But no, he talked only of sin and repentance and judgment, of the recompense of good and of evil; so they told him he was mad. They dismissed him with a polite lie, as men speak to be rid of the insane, "We will hear thee again"; and when he was gone, they chuckled and laughed and said, "The fool!"

But we need not go back to St. Paul or to Athens. We have paganism here in New York and in every other modern city. And the pagans of our day, like the pagans of ancient Athens, are always seeking some new thing. A few generations ago, it was hypnotic healing, then New Thought, then Christian Science, then the Vedanta philosophy, then the doctrine of the Yogi. After that, for a year or two, we had the "Russian stuff," as the booksellers irreverently call it. Periodically, we have spiritism. Sometimes we have Freudism, sometimes Couéism. The false philosophies follow one another in such speedy succession that one must be extraordinarily nimble to catch up, or to keep up with them. Recently the vogue was a little Frenchman, with a magic formula and a knotted string. Who can say what the next will be? Perhaps a Buddhist from Ceylon, with a prayer wheel. Perhaps a sun-worshipper from Arabia, or a Confucianist from Kiaochow. Nothing is too absurd, nothing too ridiculous, to be successful. Recently, there were twenty thousand persons gathered in the largest hall in the city of New York, listening to a lecturer speaking upon the topic, "Millions Now Living Will Never Die." But whatever be the philosophy, it must come from afar. Or if it come from near at home, it must be strange and striking and picturesque. It must be, above all things, new, or, as the "blurb" upon a New Thought book has it, "New, novel and neoteric." Whatever it be, it must not be the Gospel of Jesus Christ.

Poor, deluded, modern pagans! Why do they not understand the saying of a wise observer, "There are new things and true things, but the new things are not true, and the true things are not new." A new truth, presumably, is one that is true to-day but was not true yesterday and will not be true to-morrow. Why cannot men understand that what is true is always true? Why will they not see that what is new quickly becomes old, and that if they will have nothing that is not new, they must constantly and quickly drop one new thing to take up something newer? Why do they not understand that what is old and lives is ever new? If it had been only new, and not true, it would never have become old.

Whatever is true is always true. There is no new truth. There is no new thought. Even Christianity, the Gospel of Jesus Christ, is as old as man, as old as the world, as old as God. Christ came and revealed, or rather re-revealed, the truth that was from the beginning with God. "In the beginning was the Word, and the Word was with God." The New Testament is in the Old—in the Old by promise, in the New by actuality; in the Old by prophecy, in the New by fulfillment; in the Old by anticipation, in the New by realization. There are new discoveries, indeed, and new inventions in the physical world and the mechanical world, but there is no new truth. Truth is God, and God is eternal.

There is another criterion of truth. Truth, like God, is everlasting, and not spasmodic. Things called new are only old things that were dead and buried and dug up again. New Thought, so called, is as old as Plato. Eddyism dates back to Quimbyism, and Quimbyism to Berkeleyism, and Berkleyism is only a revival, with some modifications, of a more or less Platonic idealism. A false doctrine is preached and dies; it remains dead for hundreds of years; it is then periodically resurrected. But truth never dies. It abides forever. Novelties in philosophy and in religion come and go. But Christianity remains forever, a religion not flattering to the senses, not pampering the flesh, but, to those who apprehend it, satisfying the mind, comforting the heart, saving the soul.

BACK TO CHRIST—OR CHAOS

I

The creators of "modern civilization," though proud of the work of their hands, are strangely doubtful of its permanence. In newspapers and magazines, and on lecture platforms, the most authentic champions of modernity have been warning us of the danger of civilization's falling to pieces. True, the tone of their utterances has been a trifle less pessimistic in recent weeks, since the promulgation of the Dawes plan for saving Europe, but even yet, we are told, catastrophe is possible. Statesmen and financiers agree that one more war, coming within a generation, would ruin the world. Even without a war, conditions are such that only the wisest diplomacy will save us from universal calamity.

There is no more enthusiastic "modern" than Mr. H. G. Wells. But Mr. Wells, in spite of the characteristic buoyancy of his spirit, is gloomy about the immediate future of civilization. Not long ago he was speaking of what he called "the accelerated crumbling of a civilization." "The dykes are down," he said, "and the dark invading sea of a return to primitive things can be kept out only if all hands in unison build at the walls." Being introduced to an audience as "one who has a vision of a better world," he declared that "he saw no vision to-day save that of a world

[184]

slipping backwards." And he confessed that he looked upon this world as "a terrible and sinister world."

Almost as despondent is John Maynard Keynes, who suggests that perhaps "we have come to that point in the wheel of evolution at which science and invention can no longer help us to sustain the accelerating growth of population and comfort which before the war we had come to accept unquestioningly. We may have to curtail population or accept lower standards of life." *The Manchester Guardian*, which reports these opinions, adds, rather solemnly, "In an age of scepticism, these two men have some admitted claim to the gift of prophecy. Even if, in the manner of prophets, they prophesy evil, they may still be right."

Wells and Keynes are not the only modern prophets who unfold the scroll of "mourning and lamentation and woe." Here in America we have been deluged of late with visitors and lecturers from Europe, and almost all of them have been heralds of doom. At first we rather imagined that they were only trying to give us a bit of a fright. They had an "ax to grind." They wished us to go into the League. They wanted us to cancel their debt. Therefore, they tried to make us think that conditions over there were desperate. So we thought. But it seems that they really meant what they said. They actually anticipate the possibility of the dissolution of the entire political and social system, in Europe and in all the world.

It is an anomaly that, under these conditions, we Christians of the old tradition, who are reputed to have little sympathy for what is ultramodern, find ourselves saying to the protagonists of modern civilization "Why are ye fearful, O ye of little faith?" We have more confidence in the permanence of civilization than they. For, in truth, we are not anti-modern. Some of us at least, heartily prefer modern conditions, social, political, cultural, to any that have gone before. Certain Christians, and—we confess—certain Catholics, prefer to hark back to medieval civilization as the ideal. But it is well that the world should know that the rest of us consider a preference for the "good old days" of seven hundred years ago, to be merely an idiosyncrasy. Just as there are some non-Christians who would prefer, or think they would prefer, the Greco-Roman civilization rather than the modern, so there are Christians who think that the halcyon days of Christianity were those before the Renaissance. But in both cases the preference is merely personal. Catholicism is not officially medieval. The majority of Catholics are content to be alive here and now. With certain reservations, we are satisfied with modern civilization, and what is more, we are confident that it will not be destroyed. The basis of our confidence is, however, spiritual and supernatural. We believe that the world will not revert to barbarism, because we believe in God. We believe, not only that "God's in His heaven, all's right with the world," but we believe that God's in His world, as well as in His heaven. If He were only in heaven, the world might go to smash. But He is in the world, and His presence will save the world. Fortunately, God cannot be exiled from this world. His prophets may be driven from country to country, or even chased out of this world into the next; but any child who knows the first page of his catechism will tell you that God Himself cannot be driven away. Of course, our confidence in civilization, based upon faith in God, must seem "mystical," and perhaps superstitious, to atheists and deists. But, be that as it may, the curious fact remains that we who are presumed to be afraid of the modern type of civilization really love it better, and are more hopeful for its continuance, than are those who arrogate to themselves the claim to be "modern" par excellence.

II

I say that there are certain reservations in our approbation of modern spirit, and of modern conditions. Being generally in sympathy with the modern world, we can criticize it, good-naturedly.

Our primary criticism—not so much of modern civilization, as of those who have usurped the right to speak exclusively in its name—has been already suggested: they have made the colossal blunder of attempting to exile God. They have done this in the name of "Science," more specifically in the name of "Evolution." One of the pioneers of Darwinism was guilty of the very unscientific and quite blasphemous statement, "We have no need of the hypothesis of God." That phrase was seized upon by the half educated, who find careful and conscientious study irksome or impossible, but who dearly love a slogan. They put the smart saying, "the hypothesis of God,"

together with others like it,—"the struggle for existence," "the survival of the fittest," and "natural selection"—and imagined that they had found a substitute
for God. There is a familiar verse (poor poetry and
worse science) that expresses their opinion of the Life-
Force: "Some call it Evolution, others call it God."

I am not now concerned about the truth or falsity
of the theory of Evolution. I wish merely to accentu-
ate the fact that those who abandoned God, and put
in His place a law of Nature, or Nature itself, prepared
the way for that possible dissolution of civilization
of which there are now so many lachrymose, prognosti-
cations. If there be no God but Nature, then I admit
that the existence of civilization is indeed precarious,
and its continuance doubtful. For Nature, if she be
a deity, is a capricious deity. Nature is kind and cruel,
beautiful and terrible. Nature is sunsets and water-
falls, snow-capped mountain peaks, smiling valleys,
lakes like jewels, and rivers like streams of silver.
But Nature is more than that. Nature is cyclones,
and tornadoes, and floods, and droughts, and blizzards.
Nature is a paradise, and a jungle. Nature is an alma
mater and a savage beast. "Nature is one with rapine."
"Nature is red in tooth and claw." Nature is the lion
lying in wait for the hapless gazelle; Nature is the wolf,
tearing the lamb to ribbons.

Furthermore, Nature knows no discrimination. Calamity falls—like rain—on the just and the unjust.
The earthquake ruins churches and brothels. The
cyclone does not swerve from its path to spare invalids
or babies. When a conflagration rages, the innocent

and the guilty perish. In a storm at sea, the saint and the sinner go down together, the one praying, the other blaspheming. Nature is non-moral and cold-bloodedly impartial. Vesuvius and Mont Pelée have no pity. Fujiyama may be a deity, but it is a pagan deity, impassively cruel.

When a hurricane pursues a hundred ships running desperately before it across an open sea, catches them, tears their ribs asunder, scatters the fragments upon the ocean, or piles them up as wrecks upon the beach; when the elements, the wind, the sea, the fire, break loose in a mad riot of destruction; when the mountains open and belch forth flame and fury; when the earth trembles and tidal waves rise, and receding, suck into the maw of the ocean swarms of human beings, as a whale swallows schools of fish; irreverent men cry, "Where is now thy God?" I pass the question on to those whose only God is Nature. To the theist, the problem of evil is bewildering enough, but to the atheist, the universe must be stark mad.

If Nature be God, then God is both God and Devil. If there were no revelation of God but in Nature, we could only infer that God is more fickle and more cruel than an Oriental despot.

Those who know no God but Nature, have learned from Nature to be pitiless. The ancient Spartans killed blind babies as if they were puppies. Modern materialists would suffocate imbeciles, "Oslerize" the aged, and treat incurables with cyanide, were it not for the lingering influence of a wholly supernatural and mystical Christian tradition.

Darwin saw the logical conclusion of his theory of the "survival of the fittest." "With savages," he said, "the weak in body and mind are soon eliminated. We civilized men, on the other hand, do all we can to check the progress of elimination. Thus the weak members of society propagate their kind. No one who has attended to the breeding of domestic animals will doubt that this must be highly injurious to the race of man." [1] But Darwin never lost his Christian heart. He confessed, "The heart protests against the hard reason," and he comes to the naïve conclusion, "We must bear the undoubted bad effects of the weak surviving and propagating their kind."

Nietzsche had no such scruples. He had the courage to be logical. Knowing no God but merciless Nature, he deliberately advocated cruelty and ridiculed pity. For him the unpardonable sin was mercy. We call him mad. Unbelievers also call him mad. But they would be "stumped" if asked why they do so. If there is no God but Nature, and Nature knows no pity, why is not Nietzsche right? Nietzsche accuses his would-be atheistic fellow evolutionists of faint-heartedness, and of starting something they dare not finish.

Therefore,—to resume,—they who have gotten rid of God, and have put Nature in His place, have delivered over the universe to a capricious deity, malevolent and benevolent by turns. How can they hope to save the world, and (to use a Wellsian phrase) "salvage civilization," if a malicious and irresponsible Nature is going to smash it at any moment?

[1] *Origin of Species*, ed. 1874, pp. 149, 150.

III

Furthermore, Nature is no sufficient basis for morality. A philosopher who rejects God, and recognizes only Nature, may indeed construct a system of ethics, but if he bases his system exclusively upon what he learns from Nature, it will be a cruel system. Nature is not free. Her law is the iron law of necessity. Under such a law there can be no morality. Benjamin Kidd wrote, "All those systems of moral philosophy which have sought to find in the nature of things a rational sanction for human conduct in society, must sweep round and round in futile circles. The first great social lesson of the evolutionary doctrines which have transformed the science of the nineteenth century, is that there is no sanction in nature for human conduct. Nature as interpreted in terms of the struggle for life has no sanction either for morality or for social progress." [1]

For that reason, both morality and social progress must have a foundation in religion, or they will have no foundation at all. And when I say religion, I do not mean a devitalized "natural" religion. I mean faith in God and in a supernatural relationship between God and Man. Those scientists, therefore, and those philosophers who have abandoned God, and either have put nothing in His place, or have put Nature in His place, have done but a mean service to humanity. If there be no God and no substitute for God, there can be no sure and stable morality.

[1] Benjamin Kidd, *Social Evolution*, p. 64.

If morality be not of God, it is of man. If of man, it is only a code of customs, and customs are as changeable as styles of dress. After every great castastrophe, such as a world war, huge masses of human beings revert to barbaric or even savage customs. Men easily go "back to Nature." Civilization is not natural, but supernatural. Murder and adultery, and rape, and all manner of violence and cruelty and animalism, are natural. If there be no God but Nature, back to Nature shall we go—back to the animal, on any provocation. How, then, can there be any chance of a lasting civilization? As well profess amazement that an aviator, when something goes wrong with his machine, comes smashing back to earth, as to profess disappointment that the human race, carried aloft by civilization, comes smashing back to Nature when civilization slips a cog.

Not only disorder, but discontent, results from abolition of God. Yet those who have obliterated God from the world affect to be astonished that the world is ill at ease. But if you take away a man's food, do you wonder that he starves? If you remove the foundation stones of a building, are you amazed to see the fabric reel and topple? Why, then, pretend surprise and disappointment that man is restless and lawless, when you have removed the only source of peace and contentment—religion—and have obliterated the only authoritative Lawgiver! There is a void in the human heart that can be filled only with God. The famous sentence of St. Augustine, "Thou hast made us for Thyself, and our hearts are restless until they find rest in Thee," is no mere mystical metaphor. It is a primary fact of psychology. Why the learned have not discovered it is a riddle. They know many things of secondary importance,—the composition of the rocks, the distances between the stars, and the depths of the ocean,—but of the heart of man they remain vacuously ignorant. If they knew the heart of man, they would bring back God if only to satisfy man. Unless they bring back God, man will tear the world to pieces.

But I am speaking as if the philosophers had succeeded in banishing God. If they had succeeded, they would have reason for despair. But, in truth, they need not despair, because they cannot succeed.

The human race will never abandon God. Man is "inveterately mystical," incurably religious. Atheism is either an affectation or an aberration. The race will never be atheistic. Human beings, in the large, are no more impressed with the painfully elucubrated theories of atheistic philosophers than by the promises of chemists to feed the world on *ersatz* food. When sawdust becomes an acceptable substitute for meat, when papier-mâché serves for granite, when a marble statue turns to flesh and blood, philosophy will take the place of religion—and Nature will suffice instead of God.

Philosophy may be all very well. But philosophy must not contradict the everlasting wisdom of united mankind. The race may blunder along rather stupidly at times, but its intuitions are more nearly infallible than the constantly shifting opinions of the intellectuals. Benjamin Kidd, who saw so clearly that Nature (which he interpreted according to Darwin) provided no foundation for religion or morality, gave up religion and morality. He might better have given up Darwin. Fortunately, however, though philosophers sometimes blindly follow the scientists,—to their destruction,— the human race exercises its judgment about following the philosophers. If mankind, universally or even generally, were to accept the devastating denials of atheistic philosophy, civilization would, indeed, fall to pieces and remain in ruins. But when philosophy tries to teach men that there is no God, no good, no evil, men merely laugh at philosophy, and continue to believe in God and in morality as before, and the world is saved.

IV

Not satisfied with the attempt to abolish God, evolutionists (of the materialistic type) have declared that man has no spiritual soul. It seems we can no longer "call our souls our own." We have it in common with the brute animals. We have nothing that is exclusively human. Body and soul are both animal. In compensation for the loss of our soul, we are permitted the rather dubious privilege of calling the apes our brothers, of recognizing the repulsive baboon, the lumbering elephant, the grotesque hippopotamus as our kith and kin,—and of sharing ancestors with the hyena, the wart hog, the polecat, and the rattlesnake. Oh, sweet compensation!

Let me repeat that I am not concerned directly with the truth or falsity of this ugly theory; I am considering only its consequences. What surprises me is that the prophets of the new dispensation expect man to be moral, after they have told him that he is only animal; that they demand high spiritual perfection of him, after they have told him that he has no soul. If we who believe that man is a child of God are bewildered by man's animalism, it is not strange. But how may those who consider man only an animal blame him for animalism? If the poor fellow is only a brute, why hold up your hands in horror if he murder his brother? Do you blame a tiger for murder? If man is of one nature with the swine, why be scandalized if he wallows? If he is a reptile, why blame him for treachery? What is the sense of all your high and holy moral indignation against man, if he have no free will, if reason is only instinct, conscience an artificial acquisition, morality nothing but conformity with custom, and sin no more voluntary than the contraction of the diaphragm or the beating of the heart? If men are only animals, the world is totally a jungle, and why shall not the law of the jungle prevail? The first exponent of "*schrecklichkeit*" was not Von Kluck or Genghis Khan or Attila, but the lion in his native wilderness. If man is of one nature with the lion, there can be no such thing as inhumanity. If human beings are only beasts, humanity and bestiality are identical. So, if the materialistic evolutionists be right, warfare is our natural condition, and peace is only a breathing space between battles. Yet men like H. G. Wells, in one book, prove that we are beasts and, in another book, blame us for fighting. They lament that civilization is breaking down. Why should it not break down? If we be only animals, why may we not release the inhibitions of civilization, throw off our artificial restraints, and be our own primitive, original selves? An animal in a cage, if he hear "the call of the wild," will howl for his jungle. He may be driven into a circus ring with an iron goad and compelled to do tricks under the stimulus of a whip. But will you blame him if he finally rebels and kills his keeper? Why should he not rebel against the tyrannies of "civilized" life in a cage and a ring?

And, likewise, why should not man, if he have no soul, get "back to Nature"? If civilization is only the prodding of an iron goad, or the cracking of a whip; if our actions in human society are only like rolling a ball in a cage, or leaping through a paper hoop, why not call off the ridiculous performance, and let us all go back to our beloved freedom in the jungle? Darwin did not see the sense in this question, but Freud recognized it. If the Freudian view (the logical view for materialists) prevails, we shall no longer dread the collapse of civilization. We shall welcome it. Why, then, do the modern prophets rage so furiously together, against us poor brute beasts who have been dragged out of our jungle? If we have no soul, what can be expected of us? If there be no God, why should we attempt to act like children of God?

V

They who have taken away our souls, have also robbed us of our heaven. In its place, they offer us Utopia. But this Utopia is always a thousand years ahead of us, or, if it be contemporary with us, it is on some other planet. When Mr. Wells would introduce Barnstaple and his companions to a present-day Utopia, he was compelled by a *Deus ex machina* device to shoot them off this globe. His newest Utopia is dated so far ahead that it no longer uses Christian chronology, but it is at least 2,000 years from now. This will be small consolation to those who have surrendered their belief in an actual heaven. If there is no heaven now, there will never be one. A remote and fanciful Utopia is a poor exchange for a real and permanent heaven.

Christians whose only abiding hope in this world of woe is that of a future life of happiness, will find but cold comfort in an imaginary heaven-on-earth—or on Mars. They will read of these Utopias as they read a romance—to get away from reality for a blissful moment. But they know that Utopia is as unsubstantial as a mirage, and that a Wellsian Utopia is only the by-product of the brain of a man who sometimes attempts to write seriously, but who, being a poet *manqué*, finds the strain too great, and reverts to the romantic.

Consistent pessimists, like Bertrand Russell, know this. That is why they are (at least on paper) consistent pessimists. They consider that Mr. Wells is only a child, deluding himself with a mythological Utopia as others delude themselves with a mythological heaven. "Man," says Mr. Russell,[1] "is the product of causes which had no prevision of the end they were achieving.

[1] "A Freeman's Worship," in *Mysticism and Other Essays*. Longmans, 1918.

His hopes and fears, his loves and his beliefs, are but the outcome of an accidental collocation of atoms. No fire, no heroism, no intensity of thought or feeling, can preserve an individual life beyond the grave. All the labor of the ages, all the devotion, all the inspiration, all the noonday brightness of human genius, are destined to extinction in the vast death of the solar system. The whole temple of Man's achievement must eventually be buried beneath the débris of a universe in ruins." There is the logical conclusion of the theory that there is no future life.

VI

Lastly, the "moderns" try to get rid of Christ. Like the Sanhedrim, they sit in judgment upon Him, and they find Him wanting. Or if they do not actually judge and condemn Him, they ignore Him. They leave Him out of the affairs of the world. Our civilization is still called Christian, and is, indeed, built upon certain fundamental Christian principles, but there is little, if any, application of distinctive Christianity in the conduct of business, in the administration of justice, and in the relations of one country to another. No one representing Christ, for example, was invited to take part in the negotiations for peace at the end of the World War, or in the making of a treaty that was to prevent war in the future. Not only was the Vicar of Christ excluded from Versailles, not only were all who lay claim to be exponents of the Christian tradition ignored, but in the deliberations it seems not even to have occurred to any statesman (not even to the

idealistic Mr. Wilson himself) to make a plea that
Christian principles, rather than pagan, should be
followed.   The very mention of such a peculiarly Christian virtue as forgiveness of injuries, or such a distinc-
tively Christian sentiment as mercy to the vanquished,
would have been rejected with scorn by these peace-
makers.

The delegates were more in the mood of Shylock
than that of Portia. The most irritating word in their
ears would have been, "We do pray for mercy, and
that same prayer doth teach us all to render the deeds
of mercy." They talked "reparations" and "indem-
nities" and "mandates" for weeks on end, while the
world was falling to pieces at their feet. The highest
reach of their argument was for "justice," and, in truth,
they were entitled to justice (though again Portia might
have reminded them that "in the course of justice
none of us should see salvation";) but at no stage of the
proceedings was there any plea for merciful forgiveness.
There was no echo of Christ's "Forgive them, they
know not what they do." Understand, I do not impute
blame to the conference, or proclaim its proceedings
unjust. I simply state that its spirit was not dis-
tinctively Christian. It was conducted without reference to Christ and His gospel of mercy. And it is my
contention that the affairs of nations will never be
properly conducted until Christ is invited to sit at the
table with the diplomats—if such a scene be not
grotesquely impossible!

Even now, one is hardly considered sane if he advocates the Sermon on the Mount, or the Golden Rule,

or the general spirit of the Gospels, for the arbitrament of international controversies. Devout Christians themselves, while alleging specious reasons against introducing Christianity into treaty making, are really afraid to put the Sermon on the Mount into practice, internationally. As for the diplomats—they consider Christ a visionary. When a mild-mannered and peace-loving heathen, Mahatma Gandhi, attempted to follow Christ's words, "Resist not evil, overcome evil with good," a "Christian" nation clapped him into jail. If we had a more enlightened and better-instructed exponent of practical Christianity than Gandhi, let us say a St. Francis of Assisi, to speak to-day to kings and diplomats and congresses, he would get no more consideration than the well-meaning Hindu. Witness the treatment of the Pope, the traditional leader of Christendom. When, during the war, the Holy Father published some suggestions for peace, based upon Gospel principles, I, for one, being greatly impressed by their manifest wisdom, with a burst of enthusiasm prophesied in a great public gathering that the heads of the nations would surely invite the Holy Father, or his legate, to assist at the peace-making, when the time came. Later, while the travesty at Versailles was in progress, some one wrote, demanding that I should publicly admit that I had been mistaken.

I admitted that I had been over-optimistic,—that the Pope had been ignored,—but finally I had the melancholy satisfaction of saying, "Yes, they crowded the Pope out, and see what a pretty mess they made of the conference!"

But if it be ungracious and unwise to omit the Pope,— and all other moral leaders of the world—from an assembly designed to rehabilitate a broken civilization,— it is sheer madness to eliminate Christ, not only from such negotiations, but from all participation in the affairs of nations. There is a familiar picture by Holman Hunt, of Christ standing in the dark, lantern in hand, outside a dwelling, with the legend, "Behold I stand at the door and knock."

We, who trust in no wisdom apart from that of Christ, would say to philosophers and statesmen and diplomats, "Let Him in! You are barring out the only One who can save you." When Dante was invited to return to Florence, after being exiled, he was too proud to accept the invitation. But though the leaders of the world have shut Christ out, He will enter again if they ask Him. If they do not admit Him, their own dire prophecies of the disintegration of civilization will be realized. It is either Christ or Chaos.